LEAVING BACON BEHIND

A HOW-TO GUIDE TO
JEWISH CONVERSION

MELVIN S. MARSH

MANHATTAN
BOOK GROUP

Published by Manhattan Book Group
447 Broadway | 2nd Floor #354 | New York, NY 10013 | USA
1.800.767.0531 | www.manhattanbookgroup.com

Printed in the United States of America
ISBN-13: 978-1-960142-89-4

DEDICATION

To my grandmother, who passed away a few months before this book was published. Your memory will always be a blessing.

CONTENTS

ACKNOWLEDGEMENTS

There is an ever growing line of individuals who without them this book could not have been written.

First, Rabbi Mitch Cohen for so many things, especially his position as being the world's biggest nudnik. He contributed to several chapters where I needed experiences outside my own. Since he was also a member of my beit din, if anyone has a complaint about my Judaism, you can take it up with him. Those are his exact words.

I also would like to thank Rabbi Ron Segal and Rabbi Brad Levenberg for also helping to give me what can only be considered one of the best birthday gifts anyone could have given me. I was made an official member of "the tribe" on my birth date at my birth time. Seriously, July 18, 1981 at 9:22 a.m., I was born and July 18, 2012 around 9 a.m., I started preparing for the mikvah.

I would also like to thank Cecilia Brown, Pixie Bruner, Kathleen Bryan, Dr. Steven Chervin, Jorge Kopel, Mindy Lang, Dr. Jason Schneider, Ruth "Peaches" Friedman Scianablo, Rabbi Seth Standler, Michelle Tompkins, and Rev. Paul Turner, all of you played a part in making this book happen even if you didn't know it. I also wish to thank my ex-boyfriend, who shall remain nameless, for getting me started on this journey many moons ago.

Of course, also in the getting the manuscript to actually see the light of day, my thanks go to Jen McNabney, Madison LaCourse, and Jason Letts, plus all those unknown people behind the scenes who do the various thankless jobs, I see you and appreciate you even if I might not know your names.

For family members, well most didn't appreciate the conversion and, in fact, didn't talk to me for a while so it's hard to thank them. I would still like to thank my husband Frank Hall for not divorcing me despite me giving him every possible good reason to. Of course, we should include all the pets I've had over the past ten years who would claim that they are being ignored because I am writing and not petting them constantly. I have not neglected them, though they claim I did. (Especially don't let Corky the Corgi lie to you, he gets treats constantly and is within three feet of me at all times. He'd swear I never fed him or pet him a day in his life... he lies. He is also staring at me asking for my dinner while I am writing this. You ate, my short overweight friend, you ate!)

I, of course, want to thank all those JBCs who came before me trying to make my life at least slightly easier. I hope I do you all proud.

Melvin S. Marsh
December 9, 2022

INTRODUCTION

Hello. My name is Melvin, and I'm a Jew by Choice.

Well...actually I'm not.

While I might have chosen to make it "official" by going into the mikvah, I do not believe I chose Judaism; I believe in many ways Judaism chose *me*.

How else could one explain a connection that seemed to go beyond time and space and defy all logic? From a young age, I knew I was attached to the Jewish people in a way that I could not explain. They were my family, despite, as far as I knew, not being related biologically. How could I not love a culture and a group of people who felt more like family than my own? Of course, I would, only after conversion, find out that there were several Jewish family members in my family tree.

Despite this, it took over sixteen years (and seven rabbis) to get to the point where my conversion was officially complete. Not for lack of trying, of course, but because there were many difficult issues for rabbis to deal with that produced a barrier to conversion. These issues are mentioned throughout this book, most notably under the Special Topics section.

Hopefully, if you are reading this book, it means you are interested in learning more about conversion rituals. Or perhaps you are interested because a friend of yours is converting, you are interested in converting, you didn't previously know it was possible to convert to Judaism, or you are a student of religion and want to know more about what it is like to convert. There are any number of reasons you could be interested, and I welcome all of them.

This book is written for Jews, prospective Jews by Choice, gentiles in interfaith relationships, or for anyone with an interest in Judaism even if there is no desire to convert.

All of you are more than welcome to join me as I explain the conversion process to anyone who wishes to learn it. While this book is designed to be a resource, reference, and how-to guide for Jews by Choice, including advice I wish others had given me, this also has part of my story in it.

Why?

I am not including it because I believe my story is an intrinsically valuable one; in fact, most of the conversion books on the market simply discuss a single person or the author's journey to Judaism. This drove me crazy, because the information I was looking for (namely the nuts and bolts) weren't there. I wanted to know little things that were important to me. How does one pick a Hebrew name? What is the mikvah like? What is the naming ceremony like? How do you celebrate the Jewish holidays when you don't have any local Jewish friends or when your partner isn't Jewish? Where do you go to services when you live over an hour or more from the closest synagogue? What about if you're LGBT? Disabled? Things like that. The answers to these questions are here in this book.

For those of you who are considering converting, sometimes it can feel like the loneliest position in the world. In fact, a Jew by Choice friend of mine posted a video called "Lonely Night," a parody of "Silent Night." This loneliness is compounded, especially if you don't know other Jews by Choice and even more so if you have something that makes conversion challenging.

However, there are always going to be Jews by Choice who were previously in your position and those who are in your position now. This is why my story is included. I felt it was important for you to realize there are others like you. No matter your color, education level, sexual orientation, or where you live, you are not alone.

This is the conversion book I wish I had when I was converting. If the book had been available, I might have felt less discouraged when times were tough and would have shed fewer tears.

While I am unlikely to be present at your conversion physically, I hope learning about my journey helps and gives you strength through your own journey.

Melvin S. Marsh

EXPLORING JUDAISM

Anyone who has tried to go through the conversion process knows converting to Judaism is challenging, but it was not always so difficult. There are many converts mentioned in the Torah, and they did not have to go through as much as we do today. Abraham became the first Jew when HaShem told Abraham to circumcise himself.

Concerning the time when Abraham and Sarah were collecting people in the desert, some rabbis have argued these followers of Abraham (originally idol worshippers) should be considered among the first Jews.

Once the Israelites accepted the Torah at Mount Sinai and all of the mitzvot for themselves and future generations, there was a mass conversion, and the real Jewish nation and religion was born.

To this day, any person wishing to convert to Judaism has to go through a process similar to that performed at Mount Sinai, including mikvah, circumcision, and a sacrifice to G-d. This sacrifice would, in later years, be given at the Temple. However, as we do not have a Temple in Jerusalem currently, all sacrifices are on hold. Instead of sacrifices, many rabbis ask you to perform tzedakah.

According to the Talmud, the first Jew by Choice after Mount Sinai was Yisro (Jethro), the father-in-law of Moses' father-in-law. However, the most famous biblical figure to convert to Judaism was Ruth in the book of Ruth. When her husband, Mahlon, died, Ruth's mother-in-law Naomi encouraged Ruth to return home and remarry. Instead of leaving, Ruth replied, "Entreat me not to leave you, or to turn back from following you; For wherever you go, I will go; And wherever you lodge, I will lodge; Your people shall be my people, and your God, my God. Where you die, I will die, and there will I be buried" (Ruth 1:16-17).

By uttering those now-famous lines, Ruth becomes a follower of Naomi's religion (Judaism). Ruth was an ancestress of King David, showing that one of the most important Jews in Jewish history descended from a convert! The tradition of turning away a convert three times is attributed to Naomi turning Ruth away three times by trying to convince her to return to her own people.

There are many stories from the Torah and other Jewish writings showing the relationship between HaShem and converts and the reasons why they wished to become one with the Jewish people. In one Jewish creation myth, HaShem offered the Torah to all of the nations of the world. Individual members of each nation accepted the Torah, but as the rest of their nation did not they were not able to reach their full potential. HaShem was still not happy, as no entire nation would accept the Torah. HaShem had only one nation left, the Israelites, the smallest of the nations. HaShem was said to have frightened the Israelites by holding a mountain over their heads to convince them to accept the Torah. It is said when the Torah was offered this time, all Israelites present—as well as all of the souls of future Jews, including Jews by Choice—were present to accept it. Those souls who accepted the Torah when it was offered to their nations then were destined to join the Jewish people as Jews by Choice.

Another creation story, seen more in Kabbalah, states Jews by Choice were once born Jews, however due to a disconnection in their soul, they were reincarnated as Gentiles. They are then able to return to their people as Jews by Choice when the disconnect in their soul has been mended.

For most of Jewish history, with the exception of the reigns of King Solomon and King David, Judaism has allowed conversions (Talmud, Avodah Zarah 3B). Conversions continued to occur even after the destruction of the Second Temple and the expulsion of the Jewish people from Israel. In the Talmud, one interpretation states the expulsion from Israel was for the purpose of gaining more converts (Talmud, Pesachim 87B).

Conversions started to become more difficult around the 4th century Common Era when Christianity became the state religion of the

Roman Empire and conversion to Judaism became a crime punishable by death. However, people were still interested.

In order to assure rabbis were not converting people illegally, soldiers would disguise themselves and ask to be converted. If the rabbi agreed, the soldier would return to his unit, and the Jewish community would be destroyed. In order to protect the community while still allowing for legitimate interest, rabbis developed a tradition of turning away the convert three times. The assumption was a Roman soldier would not continue asking while someone who was truly interested would not be discouraged.

Even though conversion is no longer illegal in most areas, it is still often discouraged. Jews by Birth may tell prospective converts that conversion is impossible because it is not frequently discussed. Some rabbis are not open to working with prospective Jews by Choice at all, while others will implement the tradition of turning away the convert. Rabbis may also discourage prospective converts due to not wanting others to experience antisemitism. Discouraging conversion can happen in a variety of ways, including ignoring meeting requests, missing appointments, pointing out that you do not have to be a Jew to be a good person, or reminding you that the rules Jews must obey are stricter than the rules for Gentiles. For those who are taken on as a student, the extended process can be disheartening, but some say this is to assure the convert is sincere.

Halacha Regarding Conversion

Like any other part of Jewish life, halacha informs conversions. In the days of the Torah, it was a much simpler process than it is now. Early on, all it simply required was a circumcision, as was required of Abraham, and later a mikvah, the ritual bath.

In the Writings, specifically the Book of Ruth, it was even easier, as Ruth simply had to state her intention to follow the ways of Naomi's people. In later years, it required a circumcision for men, the mikvah, and a burnt sacrifice to HaShem. The latter was performed at the now-destroyed Temple. Now, the minimum requirements for a conversion requires a Jewish education, a circumcision for men, a panel of three learned Jews (traditionally all rabbis, although at least one rabbi is required), and three immersions in the mikvah.

After the mikvah, Jews by Choice are to be treated as Jewish by birth. It is forbidden to remind the Jew by Choice that they were not always Jewish due to the biblical commandment to love the *ger* (stranger, later translated as convert).

However, this does not always occur. Frequently, Jews by Choice are reminded they were not always Jewish or are forced to out themselves, which can be a struggle or may even be embarrassing for those who had a lengthy conversion process.

I, to an extent, do not mind discussing being a Jew by Choice or discussing my experiences in coming to Judaism. However, I do not like being outed as a Jew by Choice. The fact that my Jewish soul miscalculated and ended up being born to a Roman Catholic family is not something to be held over me.

I have even had the wives of rabbis, who should know better, discuss my conversion with other people. I was also at one point outed in a magazine as a convert, something I specifically said was off the record and had nothing to do with the story.

Further, when I was detained in Israel in 2013, the only reason I was eventually let go was because I convinced them the reason I did not attend Hebrew school as a child was because I had only been Jewish for one year! This led to more embarrassing questions, and I was treated like the scum of the Earth by the secular Israeli security person because I chose Judaism instead of being born to it.

Beginning the Journey—What Leads One to the Path of Judaism

"The journey of a thousand miles begins with one step."
—Lao Tzu

Lao Tzu's words ring just as true for spiritual journeys as secular ones. All it takes is one step, one reason to explore Judaism. There are some, like myself, who knew very young that Judaism was right for them, while others need more time to explore before coming to Judaism as an adult.

The decision to convert can be a difficult decision to make, because the hardships and stress can make anyone doubt they are on the right path, especially if the conversion takes years to finish. The truth is, for those of us who truly wish to convert, for those with a Jewish soul, nothing will stop them from joining the Jewish people.

There are many reasons you might choose to explore Judaism, particularly if you are looking to convert. One question you will be asked is, "Why Judaism?" This is a fair question, and one you need to ask yourself, as you are the only one who can answer this question and, with the exception of the rabbis who will be on your beit din (and possibly Israeli security officers), you do not have to justify your desire to anyone. Regardless, you should have an idea of why you want to convert to Judaism, even if you only admit it to yourself.

Conversion requires you to study and take on cultural practices that may be very different from what you grew up with... different holidays, different languages, different food, different rituals, and even different ways of washing your hands. Sometimes the road can be frustrating.

This is to say nothing of the antisemitism one could face. While many would like to believe that, because the Holocaust is far in the past, antisemitism is long gone. There are many positive things about being Jewish, but only you can decide what being Jewish means to you and if the journey is worth it.

Good Reasons to Convert to Judaism

A Disconnect with Religion of Birth

With as many religions as there are in the world and with spirituality being a uniquely personal phenomenon, there are many who do not connect well with the religion of their birth. Maybe there is an internal disagreement with the fundamental beliefs, rituals, or holiday practices. There could be any number of reasons. In some cases, this disconnect is so great the individual feels the need to seek out a new pathway to G-d and spiritual home better suited to them.

Desiring to Understand More About Another Religion

I have several very devout Christian friends who look to Judaism for no other reason than to more fully understand their own religion. Christianity and Islam are considered daughter religions to Judaism, and both include a form of the Torah in their sacred writings.

For Christians, their savior Jesus was Jewish, and some are interested in learning more about his life and times by studying his religion. I have met more than a few students who have come to observe services for a class project. I believe it is a wonderful thing for anyone to be willing to step out of their comfort zone and learn about another religion if the motives are pure.

Connecting with Family History

Many families can trace their history back to Jews either through direct genealogy or finding Jewish practices in family traditions, suggesting one's family might be "crypto-Jews," who practiced Judaism privately while practicing Christianity in public.

Sometimes when this is discovered, there is a renewed interest in learning more about the ancestor's religion. There are other ways to learn about possible Jewish ancestry. I have one friend who, while she already loved Judaism, learned her mitochondrial DNA (which is passed down matrilineally) was from one of the founding Ashkenazi mothers.

I have another friend who was able to trace her family history back to an exclusively Jewish location in Germany. Last I heard, she was planning to present this information to the Beit Din of America in the hopes they will issue her Jewish identity paperwork. Personally, I did not learn my family had rumored Jewish ancestry until after I converted. One rabbi I know considers the high percentage of Jews by Choice having hidden Jewish ancestry not discovered until after conversion proof the souls were always Jewish and, spiritually, were trying to return home.

Marriage or Friendship

One of the most common reasons for exploring Judaism is being engaged or married to a Jew. Gaining new family members is always a period of discovery, especially if the new family comes from a different culture or religion. Both partners should be able to understand and get along with the other partner's family, regardless of religion.

Judaism is an exceptionally family-centric faith, and members have so many wonderful childhood memories that they want their children to similarly experience. This may put family or societal pressure on the non-Jewish partner to convert or agree to raise the children Jewish. All of this requires education on the part of the non-Jewish partner and discussion prior to engaging in a committed relationship.

Perhaps, instead of Jewish family members, you have friends who are Jewish. Maybe they invited you to a Hanukkah party or a Passover seder, this piqued your interest, and you would simply like to learn more.

Living in an Area with a High Jewish Population

This can easily fall into the "friendships with Jews" section, but there is nothing stating you must be friends with Jews to want to learn more. If you are living in an area with a large Jewish population, such as South Florida or New York City, you are going to be exposed to more Jewish practices than if you lived in an area with a smaller Jewish population, such as Rocky Plains, Georgia.

For example, there might be a larger kosher section in your grocery store separate from non-kosher food, even though certified kosher food can be found in other locations in the store.

You might wonder why your children get off from school on certain important Jewish holidays, such as Rosh Hashanah or Yom Kippur, as

I did growing up despite attending public school. Simply living in a Jewish neighborhood can be quite educational!

Desire to Join a Warm Community and/or Gain a New Family

Judaism is a particularly warm religion and is very family-centric. While I know many, many Gentiles, the most unwelcoming Jew is still more welcoming to another Jew than the average Gentile.

Judaism is very clear. Always love your neighbor and welcome the stranger, as we were once strangers in Egypt. Rabbis do not attempt to scare people into coming to Shabbat services. Come. Don't come. If you join the Jewish people, you join a family who will for the most part do anything for you.

Connection to a Jewish Topic, Such as Love for Israel, or Study of the Holocaust

I have one friend who is interested in learning about the policies regarding Israel. From there, the interest expanded until he started exploring Judaism. There are many people, especially those with Nazi relatives, who converted because of a study of the Holocaust and a desire to help replenish the Jewish population.

People Having Similar Values

One thing that might attract someone to learn more about Judaism is finding out they already share similar viewpoints and/or values. Judaism is a religion steeped in rich tradition and history with a focus on ethics and education.

Some key values include a high emphasis on education (particularly the Torah), respect for women, social justice, charity, and caring for the sick and elderly. How many times in the Torah and Talmud are the orphan, widow, and stranger specifically mentioned as having special needs and warranting special attention? The answer is... a lot. Judaism is not just a religion but also a way of life.

Want a More LGBT-Friendly Religion

While the line famously used to condemn homosexuality is present in the Torah, Judaism does not make it a focus.[1] Why? There are so many reasons. For example, people may only be charged with engaging in homosexual acts if the act is performed in front of a minimum of two kosher eyewitnesses who would be willing to testify before a beit din (a religious court).

Traditionally, that would mean a minimum of two adult Orthodox Jewish men who are shomer mitzvot (keeping all 613 commandments) and who are not related to either participant would have to witness the sexual act. Those are very difficult requirements to fulfill.

Many rabbis are very supportive of the LGBT community, including many Orthodox rabbis. When Georgia was battling a very restricting anti-LGBT bill in 2015, during one rally which I was present for, the rabbi of the largest and most traditional of the liberal denominations spoke about how it was not holy to persecute the LGBT community.

A few days later, one of the Atlanta-area Orthodox rabbis said something similar. In general, provided one is not actively engaging in sexual relations in front of people, there are many Orthodox rabbis who do not consider being LGBT as a cause for concern, even though they do not promote it and might not be good at discussing the issues.

Love of Jewish Traditions and Holidays

For some, the appeal of Judaism has to do with tradition. No, I am not referring to the song from "Fiddler on the Roof," although the song has an element of truth to it. Judaism is an ancient religion and has

---

[1]   "You shall not lie with a male as with a woman; it is an abomination" (Leviticus 18:22).

managed to survive relatively unchanged to the 21st century. The same blessings over Shabbat candles, wine, and challah have been said for millennia.

We still chant ancient words of Torah in the original language every Shabbat, although some of the melodies for prayers in the service may be different. The holidays have remained relatively unchanged, although new Israeli holidays form and mark important milestones in Jewish history.

A five-hundred-year-old Haggadah (the book used for Passover Seder) at its core will be similar to one purchased last year. Many find comfort in performing rituals the same way people did in centuries past.

Belief in and Love for the Torah

An interest in and love for the Torah is another excellent reason to want to learn more about Judaism. Can learning more about the covenant between HaShem and the Jewish people and what it means to be Jewish be far behind?

Judaism "Makes Sense" or "Just Because"

There are a number of reasons why one would love and be interested in Judaism. Maybe it just makes sense to you. Maybe you cannot put into words why you feel drawn to the culture, religion, history, or people. All of these are valid reasons for wanting to learn more.

Bad Reasons to Convert to Judaism

Unfortunately, while there are many positive reasons to convert, consider converting, or learning more about Judaism, there are also negative reasons why people consider converting.

Perceived Increase in Social Status

I never considered until I read a book written by the emeritus rabbi of my congregation that this might be viewed as a reason to convert. In it, he tells a story of a husband and wife who came to services for a long time, wanted to convert, and it turned out they were expecting the Jews to give them the secret of why Jews are rich!

I do hate to break this to everyone, but not all Jews are rich. Converting will not cause you to be rich. There is no secret to becoming rich, other than to work hard. There is a higher likelihood that you will lose social status, as you will possibly lose friends and family.

Perceived to be Exciting

Skydiving is exciting. Bungee jumping is exciting. Studying for hours and hours on end and taking hours of Jewish education courses is many things, but exciting it is not. Conversion takes a lot of time and effort. You have to ask yourself many questions and completely rebuild your identity. This is a permanent change. Once it is done, it is done.

Coming Out to Your Friends and Family as a Jew

As you explore conversion, you might decide to share this with your friends and family. Certainly if you convert, some friends and family members might be curious as to why you are no longer going to church (assuming you did) or celebrating certain holidays. If some parts of your family are not expected to be supportive, you might want to find some potential allies in another part of your family and come out to them, then others one at a time.

Like any other form of coming out, you might get a variety of reactions. Your friends and family might be accepting, or they might threaten to disown or to kill you. Here are a few of the reactions I was given when I "came out" as a "Jew-in-progress." As you'll notice, none of them were particularly positive.

Reactions to Your Conversion

Why Do You Want to Become One of G-d's Chosen People Anyway?

This was asked by an old friend of mine from high school who knew me back when I started this journey. She asked me this once I started seriously pursuing it again. I don't think she could believe anyone would want to spend all this time aiming for a conversion to be the potential target of more hatred. I think that for many Jews by Choice, we would be willing to be a target in order to fulfill our rightful place with HaShem.

I Wish I Could Just Give You My Jew Card; I Don't Want It.

This was from a Jewish ex-significant other of mine who never liked being Jewish. If only the name on "the card" could have been changed to my own! I never understood why he did not like being Jewish, other than that his mother also did not like being Jewish. I always wondered why, although I have my suspicions.

G-ddamn It, What Do You Want? Do You Want Me to Convert Too?

Surprisingly, this was said by my mother after I pointed out that she was speaking Yiddish, not Dutch. As I pointed out, her religion is her own business, not mine. She had converted to Roman Catholicism as a child. I just did not want her to continue to claim Yiddish as Dutch, both of which my family can speak. She, as well as my grandmother, both know quite a bit of Yiddish and are much more conversant than I could ever hope to be.

Wait, You Mean You Aren't Already Jewish?

This came from multiple friends of mine including one who was also a Jew by Choice. The Jew by Choice and I both went to high school together and both assumed the other was born Jewish despite the fact neither of us was Jewish yet!

I Figured, Not Much of a Surprise There, or This Explains Everything

Several people mentioned some version of this response. However, I always had to wonder, what does this explain?

Do You Know What This Will Do to This Family?

This came from another family member. Honestly, I have done much bigger things potentially more disruptive to the family than converting to Judaism! There are only so many things it could do, drive us apart, bring us together. It is hard to know.

Miscellaneous Yelling

This came from more family members. Not a surprise there. The real surprise was when one of them, after she threw her fit, put a hundred dollars toward my conversion course a few weeks later.

Miscellaneous Threats

Depending on your friends and family, some may threaten you. When I was fourteen or fifteen, those threats came from my father. Luckily, he seems to have mellowed in his old age, and seventeen years after those threats started he actually sent me a holiday card and inside wrote

"Happy" and then drew a Star of David. This was after me doing every-thing possible to hide my Jewish identity and the rest of the conversion process from him and his side of the family. I still don't know how he knew, but I hope this means he has accepted it.

My Coming to Judaism Story

There are many reasons to explore Judaism, and no two individual paths will be the same. As for me, my reasons were a mixture of several of the above reasons.

My birth religion was Roman Catholicism. My father was born Catholic, and his mother was a "cradle Catholic" and very religious. My mother converted as a child along with her mother. Her mother had always wanted to be Catholic, so she converted. I knew by the age of eight that I did not believe in Christianity's New Testament. I, however, loved the stories of the Old Testament.

I also did not like how the Catholic Church treated its LGBT members, its disabled members, its members who asked too many questions, and I was not keen on the abuse scandals occurring around me. I also, at some point, realized that I did not believe Jesus was the Messiah, and I certainly did not believe salvation could only come through Jesus alone.

Jesus seemed to be just a man. Now granted, he seemed to be a very good man, but still just a man with no more or less connection to G-d than I have. After all, are we not all G-d's children? I remember separating officially from the church at the age of eight, and there is a question over whether I was officially excommunicated or not.

While Judaism certainly called to me back then, I did not want to jump to the religion that I knew second-best. After all, there might have been more suitable religions. So, instead of jumping into Judaism, I studied many forms of spirituality or really anything I could get a hold of; I had to know which was the best fit. At fourteen, I realized there were only a handful of religions that could work for me. I knew which one felt like an old comfortable sweater that I could curl up in and know I would feel safe.

Of course, one reason Judaism called to me at a young age was that I grew up in an environment with a high Jewish population... South Florida. On top of that, my parents both worked in the media industry, which as is typically regarded as also being very Jewish.

Being surrounded by Jews growing up, I was always very comfortable around them. They were for all practical purposes my extended family. I grew up with their values as my own, their friends as my friends, and in some ways their trauma as my trauma.

As far as many antisemitic Gentiles were concerned (and, yes, we still had some in Florida), I was a Jew and could be, and was, attacked. Of course, as far as the Jews were concerned I was a Gentile... granted, a very Jewish-acting Gentile, but still a Gentile.

I loved dating Jews because we had shared values, such as education and social justice, and I loved the culture. Unfortunately, I was just Jewish enough to date other Jews, but not Jewish enough to marry, as I was not Jewish under halacha.

With the rabbis rejecting me as a prospective convert as frequently as they did and for the reasons they did, I became distraught and for a time left the Jewish community. I fell in with the Wiccan community, which honored and respected me and accepted me. As much as I respected them, Wicca simply was not Judaism.

When I attended college, I never experienced so much culture shock as when I moved from a very Jewish area to a very Christian one! It took me a long time to realize that not everyone grew up being able to go to a friend's house for Hanukkah. I could not simply go to a grocery store and easily get kosher food.

My first winter away from Florida and in rural Georgia, I learned quickly that Walmart, one of the only stores in the area, had employees who did not even know what a Jew was! That was one of the loneliest experiences I have had in my entire life, and I experienced it for years. I could not find anyone else who had the customs I had.

After a very long time being away from other Jews, I realized that while I used to be a Gentile among Jews, I was now a Jew among Gentiles. I absorbed Judaism without trying to, and it simply became a part of me. I realized the only way I was going to be happy again was to rejoin the Jewish community... as a Jew.

OBTAINING A RABBI

Someone asked me, "How did you find the *right* conversion process?" She identified as half-Jewish, which I assume means she is a patrilineal Jew, although we did not discuss what being "half-Jewish" meant to her.

Personally, I do not really like the phrase half-Jewish, as it reminds me a little too much of Germany in the 1930s and 1940s. She seemed to want to be recognized by the rest of the world as fully Jewish, and I assume she figured I would be a good person to ask. In order to answer the question about how I found the right conversion process, I have to explain a little more about conversion and who is and is not considered a Jew.

If one's father is Jewish and one grows up identifying as a Jew, several denominations (Reform, Reconstructionist, and Humanistic) would accept that person as Jewish. I'm not sure if Renewal has an official position, as it seems to depend on the congregation, but I know patrilineal Jews that are considered Jewish.

The Conservative movement and the Orthodox movements would not consider this person Jewish, because Judaism is traditionally passed down through the mother; thus a patrilineal Jew would require a conversion to be accepted among more traditional movements.

Now let's talk about conversion.

Until recently, I only knew of one way to convert, the more traditional route that requires Jewish education (generally about a year), a circumcision (if male), an interview with a beit din (of three "learned" Jews), and a mikvah.

In the second process, which I learned from a series of shiurim on the topic of "Hilchot Geirut: The Laws of Conversion," a beit din is not needed so long as the person lives as a Jew among other Jews. If someone does this, they are considered Jewish by the community.

By that definition, I was Jewish long before I went before the beit din. Heck, by that definition I was almost born Jewish! Please note conversion without a beit din is an extraordinarily minor option, although one many Humanistic congregations and a few independent shuls follow, but more about that later.

Honestly, I am not sure there were truly enough options for me to be able to say, "Well this process is right for me or this is wrong for me." There were only two options! What I knew was I wanted to be considered Jewish, and there was only one way to do it as far as most Jews were concerned, as few people accept conversion without a beit din. This conversion without a beit din, by the way, is effectively a "self-conversion."

I converted in the traditional way with a beit din, because I was worried about my paperwork, and I knew that self-conversion was not the realistic path for me. One can make the argument that I was living as a Jew among Jews and thus self-converted years ago. Self-conversion is fine in certain situations, such as if you are only doing it for yourself.

However, as one of my beit din members said when he handed out the certificate of completion for our introduction to Judaism course, "Nothing in this religion happens without a certificate." And that is very true.

Having your "papers" (or evidence of your parents' papers or your maternal grandmother's papers) can be very important for joining a synagogue, making aliyah, getting married, or really having almost any life cycle event. As a Jew by Choice, my only paperwork identifying me as a Jew is my conversion certificate.

Jews who "self-convert" do not get issued conversion papers. In addition, since there is no evidence a conversion took place, it can be hard to prove the person did what was asked of them and that they really are Jews rather than Noahides or even Gentiles pretending to be Jewish! I wanted my paperwork for the purposes of moving to Israel (just in case) or marrying a Jew (just in case). I also figured since I had been studying for conversion for such a long time that I deserved my paperwork.

Prior to joining the congregation that finally converted me, I was in an independent group that to some extent followed the "Live as a Jew, you are a Jew" rule. However, I hated being called a Jew before I was "official" and my paperwork was issued. I felt it was a lie, since I had not gone to the mikvah yet.

However, when I went before the beit din, one of my final statements discussed what I had learned about conversion without a beit din. As I told them, "It really doesn't matter how you rule, because very little is going to change; I am still going to live as a Jew because I AM Jewish." Not long after that, everyone ruled in my favor.

If I had been a patrilineal Jew, been raised Jewish, had Jewish identity paperwork, or could get identity paperwork, my choices might have been different. I would have been accepted as Jewish by at least some movements and would have been less likely to consider conversion to Conservative or Orthodox Judaism unless I had to do so for the purposes of marriage.

How to Pick a Sponsoring Movement

One of the big choices you are going to have to make before you convert is deciding on a sponsoring movement. There are four main movements (Orthodox, Conservative, Reform, and Reconstructionist) and minor movements including Renewal and Humanistic. The ultra-Orthodox community generally does not convert but instead sends their prospective Jews by Choice to the Modern Orthodox community for conversion.

Traditional Judaism, a term that will occasionally be used, is very similar to Orthodox Judaism, except the men and women often sit together. Messianic Judaism will not be discussed as, despite the name, they are not considered a branch of Judaism even though many have Jewish ancestry.

Depending on the size of the Jewish community where you live, you might not have a choice, since there might be only one or two synagogues. Alternatively, there might not be any synagogues in your area. Assuming you have an option, you will need to consider which movement is the best fit for you.

Each movement is somewhat different regarding their prayer services, their position in regard to halacha, and even the function of the rabbis, etc. One way you might have an idea of which is best for you is to go "shul shopping" and attend different services at different synagogues. Attending different synagogues and different services is a good way to find out which synagogue or service you are most comfortable with.

Types of Synagogues

Orthodox

Of all the movements, the Orthodox movement is the most strict and most observant. The Orthodox believe the Torah is the literal word of G-d and the 613 mitzvot are binding. Men and women are separated in synagogue services, generally with a mechitza dividing the sexes.

Modesty, particularly among women, is strongly encouraged. Skirts are worn and clothing must cover the elbows. Married women will often keep their hair covered when out in public. It is not uncommon for men and women to avoid touching one another unless they are close family. Services are often very long and have extensive amounts of Hebrew. Halacha, the Jewish law, is unchanging over time.

This movement is considered the most difficult to convert to. The education required before one goes to the beit din and the mikvah may require a few years of lessons and is likely to be the most extensive. Often, as I have heard from Orthodox Jews by Choice, Orthodox rabbis will not only require a potential Jew by Choice to move to an area where there is a very large Orthodox Jewish population but also to move within walking distance to a synagogue.

One benefit to converting Orthodox is that all other movements will accept the conversion should you decide later that you do not wish to be Orthodox. The Orthodox also tend to assume prospective Jews by Choice have an Orthodox family who are able to act as mentors. These mentors can be very helpful in order to assure one learns how to live an observant lifestyle.

If moving to Israel is important to you and you wish to be allowed to marry in Israel or be buried in Israel, Orthodox might be the most appropriate. Non-Orthodox converts can move to Israel but might be denied the right to marry—although times are changing.

There are a few negatives to pursuing an Orthodox conversion. As previously mentioned, the long education time and possibly being required to move might be financially prohibitive for you. While Orthodox rabbis will generally recognize other Orthodox conversions, this is not always the case.

Further, some rabbis will hold the certificate of conversion for a period of time in order to assure that the Jew by Choice continues to live Jewishly after the conversion. If you are LGBT, conversion will be more difficult with this movement. Notice, I said more difficult, but not impossible, as there are a few rabbis who will arrange for conversions even if one is transsexual. In Tel Aviv, Israel there is even an Orthodox LGBT synagogue!

Conservative

The Conservative movement has many similarities to the Orthodox. The Conservative movement views halacha as binding. However, Conservative Jews believe halacha can be adapted to fit a more modern Jewish life. For example, while the Orthodox will not drive on Shabbat, Conservatives will allow driving to the synagogue on Shabbat assuming it is too far to walk.

There are some differences. The Conservative movement is more egalitarian, and there are female rabbis, while the Orthodox do not ordain female rabbis. If I am not mistaken, the Conservative movement recently ordained its first openly gay rabbi.

Men and women can sit together at the services if they wish, and women can read from the Torah scroll. Conservatives will accept most liberal conversions assuming all of the requirements (circumcision, beit din, and mikvah) are met.

However, there can be a wide range of observance levels depending on the individual synagogue and the community it serves. In the community where I converted, the mikvah used for non-Orthodox conversions was housed in a Conservadox synagogue, so named as it was on the border of Conservative and Orthodox.

There were several ways you could tell it was on the border. In the restrooms, there was tissue paper instead of normal toilet paper, and this was to prevent someone from tearing paper on Shabbat. Further, they boasted that the synagogue is within an eruv (a ritual enclosure), so their observant members don't have to worry about violating Shabbat by carrying an item in a public domain. Further, while there was a very large mixed-seating section, for those who were uncomfortable sitting with members of the opposite sex, there was also mechitzot (plural of mechitza) on each side, allowing for single sex seating, if desired.

There are other Conservative synagogues that are less observant, do not offer single sex seating, do not stress the importance of mikvah, do not mind if you carry outside of the eruv on Shabbat, and have normal toilet paper in their restrooms.

Some Conservative synagogues do not have separate kitchens or at the least separate utensils for the preparation of meat versus dairy dishes. There is a higher rate of intermarriage among the Conservative movement than there is among the Orthodox and, depending on the synagogue, they could be anything from welcoming to interfaith couples to actively considering them a threat to Judaism.

The benefits of a Conservative conversion include a shorter time period than an Orthodox conversion. All other liberal branches of Judaism will accept a Conservative conversion.

For the negatives, the conversion is not considered valid according to most Orthodox rabbis. There might be individual rabbis who accept the conversion, but this is rare. As a general rule, converting Conservative and then starting to attend an Orthodox synagogue or such will require a second conversion. Further, like with the Orthodox, LGBT individuals might have difficulty being comfortable, but this depends on the community. Their conversion request might even be denied simply due to being LGBT or it might be welcomed.

Reform

The Reform movement is, by far, the largest of the liberal movements of Judaism. It is also the oldest, having been founded in 19th century

Germany. In fact, this was the first movement to separate from what we now call Orthodoxy. With a significant amount of the world's Jews identifying as Reform, it is very likely that if there are only one or two synagogues in your area that one of them will be a Reform synagogue. Reform will accept all conversions performed by most other liberal movements.

Like the Conservative movement, the Reform movement believes traditions should be modernized. Men and women sit together and women are frequently called up to the Torah. Women represent a little less than half of currently ordained Reform rabbis, although they currently represent a majority of rabbinical students. The Reform movement also includes many LGBT rabbis.

Halacha is considered non-binding, although is often interpreted as a set of general guidelines or suggestions on how to live. This interpretation of halacha often transfers the responsibility from the rabbi to the individual. While the rabbi might offer a suggestion, individuals decide how halacha applies to their lives and which mitzvot are going to be followed and how.

While it is traditional to cover one's head in a service and wear a tallit during morning services, some Reform men will choose to go bare-headed and go without a tallit. Women, on the other hand, may cover their head with a kippah during services and may even wear a tallit if they desire. Any of the options are acceptable in a Reform service, although individual synagogues might require a head covering if one approaches the bima from which the Torah is read.

Reform, as well as Reconstructionist, also accept patrilineal descent. Thus, the child of a Jewish father is considered Jewish even if the mother is not. In more traditional branches of Judaism, the mother's status determines whether or not the child is Jewish. The interpretation of halacha as being "non-binding" can put Reform and Orthodox at odds with each other particularly in regard to conversions.

Reform synagogues and their services vary from being on the Conservative/Reform border ("Reform toward Traditional") to being almost assimilated into, and becoming no different from, Gentile society. There are services where there is very little Hebrew and there are others where there is a significant amount of Hebrew. Some synagogues will only offer kosher meals, while others do not. Generally, all Reform synagogues are welcoming to interfaith couples, minorities, LGBT couples, etc.

The benefits to converting Reform include its accessibility. As the largest movement of liberal Judaism, there are synagogues all over the United States and throughout the world, so there is likely one near any prospective Jew by Choice. When attending a synagogue for the first time, Reform might feel more welcoming and less intimidating.

During the conversion process, depending on the rabbi, the course of education might be shorter than the traditional year-minimum required. Further, some rabbis might not require parts of the traditional conversion process, such as circumcision or mikvah, although these things are strongly encouraged.

The Conservative movement will generally accept Reform conversions provided all parts of the traditional conversion process are met (education, beit din, circumcision, and mikvah), although this is a case by case basis. Reconstructionist, Renewal, and Humanistic will also accept Reform conversions. The state of Israel will allow Reform Jews by Choice (who converted outside of Israel) to be granted aliyah.

The negatives to converting Reform primarily relate to who accepts the conversion. Not all Reform conversions are accepted by the Conservatives. Additionally, Orthodox rabbis will not generally accept the conversion. However, there are individual Orthodox Jews who will accept Reform conversions on a case by case basis, such as if you are very observant, but that is so rare that one should never count on that. In Israel, Reform and Conservative Jews are considered secular Jews and are not allowed to marry or be buried in the state of Israel. Further, it was only very recently that a small number of Reform and Conservative rabbis were recognized as rabbis by the state of Israel.

Reconstructionist

Another liberal branch of Judaism, and the last, smallest, and youngest of the four main movements, is the Reconstructionist movement. Although Reconstructionism officially split from the Conservative movement, it tends to have more in common with the Reform movement.

Halacha is considered non-binding, however the position is it should be upheld as an important part of Jewish culture, only to be disregarded if there is a reason to do so. Reconstructionist congregations will accept all conversions and accept patrilineal descent.

The benefit to converting Reconstructionist is their welcoming attitude toward the LGBT community and interfaith families. Further, they are in some ways the most pioneering of the movements. Reconstructionist Judaism was the first branch of Judaism to not only ordain women but also to ordain gays and lesbians.

The negatives concern accessibility and who will accept the conversion. As one of the smallest movements, finding a Reconstructionist synagogue might be a challenge, as they are primarily found in areas with larger Jewish communities. Like with Reform conversions, the Conservative movement might not accept all Reconstructionist conversions unless it meets Conservative standards. The Orthodox will not accept the conversions.

Renewal

Meditation, dance, chant, and mysticism have been present in Judaism since the beginning, but they have recently experienced a renewal and increase in practice. Renewal Judaism is more focused on this mystical aspect. Although the teachings of Jewish Renewal are often found in classes taught by other denominations, the relatively small number of synagogues affiliated with the Jewish Renewal movement makes it a relatively minor movement. Of Renewal-affiliated rabbis, many are also affiliated with another movement.

The benefits of converting with a Renewal rabbi include a unique approach to spirituality and a Judaism blended with invigorating spiritual practices that are rarer among other denominations. This denomination has always, to me, seemed like the most fun of all of them.

The negatives include accessibility. There are very few Renewal specific synagogues, so finding one might be a challenge. The Orthodox will not accept the conversion, however other liberal branches likely will, although there is no guarantee.

Humanistic

Started in the 1960s, Humanistic Judaism is a small movement based out of the United States. Instead of focusing on Judaism as a very distinct set of beliefs in G-d, it values and stresses Jewish identity through participating in Jewish culture and learning the history of the Jewish people. Due to its relative lack of reference to G-d, it is also called "G-d-optional Judaism" or "Atheist Judaism." Humanistic Jews continue to celebrate their identity and participate in Jewish holidays and life cycle events.

Despite the fact many Jews do not recognize this branch of Judaism, I feel nothing but respect for it, which is why I am including it. One of the reasons I like the movement is because it is very simple to join. They define a Jew as someone who identifies with Jewish history and culture and is going to be a part of a Jewish future. By their movement's standards, I was Jewish long before the mikvah.

I identified with Jewish culture and history and am willing to work to build a Jewish future. I think understanding what their movement's position was helped me be able to utter the words "I am Jewish" before I went to the mikvah. When discussing the movements of Judaism in my conversion course, I was the one to mention that Humanistic was absent from the list. When told Humanistic Judaism was not "real" Judaism, I mentioned I learned more about what it was like to be Jewish from a Humanistic podcast than any of the Reform or Conservative podcasts I listened to.

Due to the lack of support and recognition this movement receives from other movements, there are very few benefits to converting with this movement. However, on the other hand, there are also no real negatives outside of a strong likelihood that your conversion will not be recognized elsewhere. Their conversion is, as far as I can tell, more like an adoption by the congregation. You can identify as Jewish all you want, but few mainstream movements will accept your "adoption." Regardless, I have learned some valuable life tips from members of this movement.

How I Came to My Decision

Over sixteen years and seven rabbis, I approached all mainstream movements of Judaism. I approached Conservative, Orthodox, Reform, and Reconstructionist. I even approached a post-denominational rabbi. At first I was being taught Conservative (Conservadox) Judaism, however I was too modern in many ways for the rabbi.

I loved tradition and had an internal sense that Conservative toward Orthodoxy fulfilled my need for traditions and rituals while giving me the structure I enjoy living by. However, I was (and remain) pro-LGBT, pro-women, and had gender-variant behaviors that did not sit well with the rabbi. If I had had access to a Conservative rabbi who was a little more lax, I might have been able to convert Conservative. A few years after that, I met an Orthodox rabbi who attempted to charge me three times more than I made that year in order to convert me. That was the cost to "overlook" the problems seen in me.

However, the more appropriate place for my opinions was with either Reform or Reconstructionist, who were less likely to object. Of those two options, I preferred the idea of going Reform. However, no fewer than five people told me that I had to speak with the local Reconstructionist rabbi. We worked together for a few months, and, to put it mildly, we had a major disagreement and realized we could not work together. I met others who had similar problems with the same rabbi.

This left Reform. I was perfectly happy with this option, as I considered myself Conservadox in practice but Reform in my opinions regarding the value and equality of other human beings. While I disagree with the Reform position on patrilineal descent and would certainly prefer to see others fulfill more mitzvot, I am a strong supporter of the Reform position on the value of women, the support of the LGBT community, and many other key values.

While I was in the process of conversion, I met a wonderful woman through a social networking site. I had to warn her in Yiddish that the person she was talking to, a mutual acquaintance, was a bit antisemitic, so she had to be careful. When my conversion attempt with the

Reconstructionist failed, this wonderful woman put me in contact with her nephew, a Reform rabbi, who convinced me to not give up.

Despite him calling me a Conservative Jew due to my position on kashrut, he listed a few of his friends who were rabbis at Reform synagogues a few hours from my house. I looked at the three and approached the rabbi at the shul that looked the most LGBT-inclusive. He took me on, and a few months later, on my birthday, I had my date with the mikvah.

Despite undergoing a Reform conversion and attending a Reform shul, for all practical purposes I live as a Conservative to Conservadox Jew, although a few people have stated that if I were any more traditional in how I perform some of the mitzvot I would be Orthodox. My house is mostly kosher, and I keep several sets of dishes, meat, dairy, and a set of non-kosher dishes just in case so Gentiles do not have to worry about which set to use.

Pork and shellfish are banned from my house completely, although I do eat things that may not have a hechsher if all the ingredients should be kosher otherwise. I light my candles every Shabbat and roughly every other Shabbat I go "shomer Shabbat," which is observing Shabbat in such a way that none of the thirty-nine categories of work forbidden are violated, to such an extent that an Orthodox friend has made comments on it. Some of those things are as mundane as not turning on (or off) a light or even cooking.

Personally, I think this is one of the reasons I have had several Orthodox Jews (including a Hasidic Jew) accept my Reform conversion when I know they have not accepted other Reform conversions. I have been known to quote Talmud and discuss my opinions on halacha in the modern time, usually taking a more traditional viewpoint. I frequently take online Yeshiva classes taught by Orthodox rabbis.

However, I also love to read about Jewish Renewal at every opportunity. Of all the movements, I have more Renewal books than anything else. I enjoy a psycho-spiritual approach to Judaism.

Despite all this, if given the choice between having to choose between attending a Reform synagogue or attending a Conservative synagogue for the rest of my life, I would likely choose Reform due to its more welcoming nature. I would rather be the most observant member of a Reform shul and be happy, than to be an average member of a Conservative shul and be unhappy and feel unwelcome. Yet I enjoyed my time in LGBT friendly Orthodox synagogues, so it may be specific to the individual places I have been.

Finding a Rabbi

One of the most important things before you convert will be to find a rabbi to serve as your sponsoring rabbi. Without a rabbi to sponsor you and issue you paperwork, it is difficult to convert or to later prove a conversion occurred. There are many ways to try to find a rabbi you can work with. If they are less than enthusiastic about conversion, approach them at least two more times, as it is tradition to turn away prospective converts.

As you look for rabbis, there are things you might want to consider. You might not want to work with the first rabbi you meet if you do not feel as if you are compatible or that this will work out.

Here's an important question to ask yourself. Does the rabbi seem to have time to work with you? Rabbis are very busy, and no matter how much they might want to work with someone, they simply might not have the time. This is a sad state if this is the case, however, some rabbis will explain the situation and might refer you to a different rabbi or try to make the time for you.

Does this rabbi have the ability to work with you? One assumes the rabbi knows the Jewish component, however this does not mean both of you can work easily with each other. If the rabbi does not have a lot of experience with conversion or Jews by Choice, perhaps this rabbi might not be the right one for you.

Do both of you get along personality wise? If there is friction between the two of you due to conflicting personalities, it might be better for you to consider not using that rabbi even if he (or she) has available time to schedule. A rabbi who makes things difficult on you and who you cannot work with might be worse than a rabbi who is very nice but may not have the time for regular meetings.

Do you feel that the rabbi is a good teacher? One of a rabbi's jobs is to teach. A prospective Jew by Choice might have many questions on the road to conversion. Some of these questions might be difficult to answer, so it would be best to have a teacher who is able to explain things clearly. Now not every rabbi is a skilled teacher in all matters, so it is possible that you might have several teachers, but your rabbi should be one of them.

You also have to be on the same page with your shared expectations for the process. Some rabbis, not most, might ask you to move physically closer to the synagogue. Some, particularly the more traditional ones, might require you to live within the eruv if there is one in your area. Some might expect you to come to each and every service. If these things do not work for you, then you might wish to interview another rabbi.

Here are some suggestions on how to find rabbis.

References from Family or Friends

One way you can find a rabbi is through friends and family. Conversion is a very personal business, and one can even argue that finding the right rabbi can be like looking for a spouse. Have your friends and family suggest rabbis that they know and who might be willing to work with prospective Jews by Choice. Ask other Jews by Choice about their experiences and their opinions of rabbis in the area. Some rabbis might be more suited and open to discussing conversion than others.

I indirectly used this route in what could be the most arguably unusual case of Jewish geography in the world. A "friend's" antisemitic comments on Facebook led me to become good friends with another person whose nephew was a rabbi in Texas. The nephew was able to introduce me to a former classmate based in Atlanta, about two hours from my house, who would become my converting rabbi.

Attending Services

Another route is to "shul-shop" and attend a variety of synagogues until you find the synagogue with the services you like the best. Then approach one of the rabbis at that synagogue. This allows you to get a feel for the rabbi's style before you officially meet them.

Cold Contact

One other option is to find the contact information for every local synagogue and simply try to make an appointment with each rabbi, even if you have never attended services at their synagogue. I am not sure this is the best option. However, for some people, they don't have a choice. I had to do this as well to meet with others.

Distance Conversion Courses

There are rabbis who provide distance conversion courses, and when you are finished you travel to their location and go before the beit din. Not all of these courses are legitimate, and I had one Orthodox rabbi who tried to swindle me for five thousand dollars. One of my beit din members knew of that rabbi and believed he should be thrown in jail. There are however legitimate distance programs, although they are few and far between. This should be a last resort.

Meetings with the Rabbi

At the First Meeting

The very first meeting you have with a rabbi will be more like a "getting to know you" session. You might be asked about your previous experience in Judaism. You might be asked about what you have or have not studied. You might be asked what your strengths are or what your weaknesses are. For me, I always told them I was raised in South Florida, all my friends were Jewish, that I had been wanting to convert since I was fourteen, and then how many rabbis I, at that point, had been rejected by, which usually brought on the question as to why I was rejected by each, which I then answered.

You might be asked why you want to convert. Be honest about why. If you have a Jewish significant other, say so. The rabbi might be more upset if that information comes out later. People were always surprised that my partner was not Jewish.

Given the importance of circumcision, men might be asked if they were circumcised. One rabbi asked me twice, because he forgot the answer the first time. Men might be informed of the importance of circumcision, if not circumcised, and the importance of the haf dam brit if already circumcised.

You might even be persuaded not to attempt the conversion process for any number of reasons. This could be legitimate, or it could be part of the traditional turning away of the prospective Jew by Choice, which generally occurs three times in order to assure you are sincere.

You might be asked about the challenges you might face when converting. Is your family supportive? Are your friends? Have you already tried to live a Jewish life? Do you live far away from a synagogue? Is keeping kosher going to be a problem? What about Shabbat? Do you have a disability that will require special accommodations?

This is also the time to ask the rabbi questions about what he feels about the entire converting process. What the expectations are for Jews by Choice, etc. These are important things to know before you can be assured that this rabbi is the one that is best to work with you.

At the Second Meeting and Beyond

Assuming all goes well, both of you are suitable toward each other, and the rabbi agrees to take you on as a student, there will be many more meetings. The meetings will include topics such as the conversion ceremony and the education you must complete before the conversion.

Generally, the primary education will occur in an introduction to Judaism class and may include secondary individualized supplementation. The individual portion, your secondary education, could include almost any form of outside activity such as visiting a Holocaust museum, watching movies, attending Jewish life cycle events, attending lectures, additional Hebrew classes, or other ways to develop a Jewish identity. This is up to your rabbi's discretion. In my first meeting with my converting rabbi, I was told there was going to be secondary supplementation, then I sent him a list of all the things I already did. It must have satisfied him as he did not ask me to complete more.

For my converting rabbi, we probably spent more time working on how to perfect my spiritual autobiography and Hebrew than anything else. We spent an entire hour just on the blessings, because I am not nor have I ever been comfortable in Hebrew, and I asked him to help with the one thing I was worried about the most.

Depending on your rabbi, you might be asked to meet with different members of your beit din. This was not required of me, since I knew two of my beit din already and asked to meet with the third just so I could know who he was. I ended up becoming very close with "Mysterious beit din member 3" as I would later call him.

When all of these meetings are complete, you are going to eventually pick a date for the ceremony, which we will talk about later.

ACQUIRING A JEWISH EDUCATION

You may start your education long before you meet a rabbi, or you might even meet your rabbi through a class. You may have an extensive amount of prior learning before you even join a class, or you might know very little. However, most rabbis will want you to join an introduction to Judaism course or otherwise show equivalent knowledge. There are many ways for you to find this course.

Family or Friends or Other Jews by Choice

Like searching for a rabbi, it is possible that your friends or family might know of conversion courses. However, it is more likely that another Jew by Choice would be able to point you in the correct direction. I have referred prospective Jews by Choice (and interested Christians) to introduction to Judaism courses offered by the non-profit organization where I took my last course.

Local Jewish Community Center

Your local Jewish Community Center is likely to have their fingers on the pulse of the community and know the courses being offered. Many times, they offer the course themselves.

Rabbi Referrals

Most rabbis will refer you to courses that either they are actively involved with or have teachers they respect. I volunteered with a Jewish non-profit where rabbis referring students was the number one source of students. Going to a school recommended by your rabbi has an added benefit. If the rabbis trust the teacher of the course they referred you to, the rabbis you are working with can focus on a separate part of your education. If you complete the course before you meet with a rabbi and thus already have the completion certificate, you might be able to speed through part of the process.

Internet Research

Simply by performing a search on your favorite search engine, you might be able to find a local Jewish conversion course. When I was ready to start looking, I searched "Jewish conversion Atlanta" (without quotes), I found an introduction to Judaism course that was about to start, and they were just perfect for me to join.

Internet Programs

Like with finding a rabbi, there are internet-based conversion courses. Some of them are more legitimate than others. When in doubt, consult other rabbis as well as ask about communities dedicated to Jews by Choice.

Topics You Will Need to Know About

There are many things that could be covered in your conversion course and what your rabbi specifically requires of you could vary.

Hebrew

As much as I would love to say you can convert without knowing any Hebrew, I think a basic knowledge of the Hebrew alphabet can go a long way. I am horrible with foreign languages, even languages related to English and using the Latin alphabet. I told people I would do anything, but please, please no more Hebrew. After all, Hebrew is written from right to left and is in another alphabet! To complicate matters, some letters are always silent, many times there are no vowels, you have to learn what some words are by context, and there are different pronunciations with Ashkenazi versus Sephardic Hebrew.

At the very least, one should try to become familiar with the basic letters and what sounds each make. Writing English words in Hebrew letters can help and is the best way I have found to try to learn the letters. For spoken Hebrew, I am a fan of Pimsleur's Modern Hebrew program, although it is expensive. I am also a fan of using websites such as Quizlet and Memrise to learn vocabulary.

Jewish Beliefs

Although you might already think you know Jewish beliefs, this is an important and central part of the curriculum. Unfortunately, since different movements have somewhat different beliefs, this section could be watered down to only reflect what Jewish beliefs have in common, such as being monotheistic, or could be very detailed about what the different movements believe, or you might only learn what your movement believes. This section will also include going over the different holy books such as the Torah, Prophets, Writings, and Talmud. Hopefully, this would include ethics as well as the concept of mitzvot and holiness.

Prayer

An observant traditional Jew prays multiple times a day and, ideally, offers at least a hundred blessings a day. In all likelihood, you will not learn all the blessings one could potentially perform. However, the role of prayer is important, as is the role the synagogue plays in Jewish life. Ideally, you should also be walked through several services prayer by prayer, although it is also important to realize that, with the exception of a few prayers that require a minyan, most prayers can occur at home.

Laws of Kashrut

While this could just as easily be wrapped into the above section on Jewish beliefs, I find the laws of Kashrut to be detailed enough that they should be considered separately. While you may or may not be expected to keep kosher, it is important to understand the details. While kashrut is partially ethical, in that the pain to the animal is minimized, it is also in part a national "Jewish" law.

Kashrut is one of many things separating the Jewish nation from other nations. You will learn the difference between biblical kosher (the laws set forth in the Torah about not eating pork, shellfish, and non-kosher animals) and rabbinical kosher, which specifies no mixing of milk and meat, the waiting time, and how one kills the animal correctly. You will also continue to learn about hechshers.

Jewish History

As a people, Jews have been around a very long time and archaeologically the evidence supports thousands of years of history. In order to join a people, it is important to know their past in order to become a part of their present and their future. There is so much information on Jewish history, one could study it for years and still learn more information.

Antisemitism

For as long as there have been Jews, there has been a history of antisemitism. Mostly, you will learn this throughout the history portion of the course. You will, in particular, learn about the Holocaust and you may have the opportunity to visit a Holocaust museum or listen to a Holocaust survivor speak.

Given the history of antisemitism, it is important to learn because, as Jew by Choice, you will be targeted just like any other Jew. In fact, you are likely to become a target of antisemitism before you are officially Jewish! I have known several people on track to become Jews by Choice who decided they could not deal with the antisemitism and stopped the process.

Israel and Zionism

The frequent attacks on the state of Israel should give any Jew, born Jew or Jew by Choice, cause for concern. In order to understand Jews, you have to understand Israel, and in order to understand Israel, you have to understand Jews. This history and connection of the Jewish people to Israel is an important one given the foundational principles of Israel.

Israel is more than a country (the State of Israel). It is the land (Eretz Israel), it is also the nation of Israel (the Israelites who then became the Jewish people), and it is the location of the holiest sites in Judaism, as the Temples were there. Of course, Israel is also a person too, as Jacob was renamed Israel! Upon conversion, you enter into the nation of Israel, and after a set period of time, I believe it is a year in your converting community, you are able to immigrate to Israel under the Right of Return.

Lifecycle Events

Jewish tradition is filled with rites of passage. The first tradition would be a B'rit Milah (bris/circumcision) and baby naming for a baby boy or a baby naming ceremony for a baby girl, this tradition of baby-naming welcomes babies into the Jewish nation. To mark a passage into religious adulthood, a bar mitzvah (for boys at age thirteen) or bat mitzvah (for girls age twelve) ceremony are usually held, although the child becomes a religious adult even if the ceremony is not performed. This topic of lifecycle events could also include Jewish weddings, Jewish funerals, and death rites, as well as conversion.

Jewish Calendar and Holidays

If one is going to live as a Jew, one needs to have a basic understanding of the Jewish calendar. A new day starts at sunset (as according to Genesis it was night before day), and Shabbat is the last day of the week. The calendar is lunar-based with the new moon symbolizing the first day of a new month, while the full moon occurs on the fifteenth of the month.

There are leap months (Adar I) to keep the Jewish calendar on track, and there are four different New Years for different things (New Year of Kings, New Year of Cattle, New Year of the World/Calendar Year, New Year of Trees). There are also countless holidays, including Shabbat, Days of Awe starting with Rosh Hashanah and ending with Yom Kippur, Sukkot, Shmini Atzeret, Simchat Torah, Hanukkah, Tu B'Shevat, Purim, Passover, Counting of the Omer, Lag B'Omer, Yom HaShoah, Yom HaZikaron, Yom HaAtzma'ut, Yom Yerushalayim, Shavout, and the three weeks of mourning leading up to Tisha B'Av! This is not including several additional fast days such as Tzom Gedaliah, Asara B'Tevet, Ta'anit Esther, Ta'anit Bechorot, and Tzom Tammuz!

Additional Education, Experiential Learning, and Living a Jewish Life

There are additional aspects of Jewish education and Jewish life that might be required of you depending on the rabbi. All of these are generally found outside of the primary conversion course itself, although some may be included as part of the curriculum.

Attend Shabbat Services

This is important less for the education it can provide and more for the sense of community and Jewish identity that will develop. Yes, it is important to attend services in order to become more comfortable identifying as a Jew. Yes, having that shared experience can bring you together as part of the community.

It would also help to allow you to become more familiar with the prayers that many born Jews know, even if they do not use them regularly. These would be blessings such as the candle-lighting, HaMotzi (blessing over bread) and Kiddush (special blessing over wine for Shabbat and holidays).

Some rabbis will allow you to stream services if you are very far from a synagogue. I was able to stream live (and sometimes completely interactive) independent, Reform, Conservative, and Humanistic services. It was not until I was already Jewish when I was able to attend my first Orthodox service. (Sadly, it was a shiva minyan.)

Attend Additional Classes and Additional Tutoring

Several years before my official introduction to Judaism course, I was privately tutored in Judaics from a Conservadox point of view. My weekly totals were between twelve to fifteen hours a week during the school year and over twenty hours per week during the summer. I was tutored in everything from Hebrew to Talmud and covered many more subjects than we did during my introduction to Judaism course. This allowed me to come in with a good foundation on which to further my education.

After my official introduction to Judaism was over, but before I went to the mikvah, I took the next course in the sequence. This course went into several new subjects that were not discussed in as much depth. Then I took the third in the sequence. I also paid for a para-rabbi course, which I have not yet completed.

I also took shiurim through an online yeshiva and studied everything from Talmud to Halacha to Kabbalah to laws specifically relating to those regarding conversion. Furthermore, I also took individual classes offered online and in-person such as courses on the Talmud and even a course about "Being Jewish Alone."

Attend Jewish Cultural Events

Cultural events could include everything from lifecycle events to museums. Where I grew up, there was a theater that put on plays with Jewish themes or by Jewish writers. Many large metropolitan areas also offer Jewish Film Festivals where there are dozens or even hundreds of films that are screened over the course of a few weeks in participating theaters. If movies are not your thing, there are also Jewish music festivals and Jewish book festivals.

Another option is attending a Holocaust exhibit or visiting a Holocaust museum. There are also options to hear survivors or their children speak about their experiences during the Holocaust. While this can be a sad subject, it is important to hear about the antisemitism and what Jews went through.

You can also attend Jewish lifecycle events if you are invited. While you might not be invited to a bris in someone's home, you might be able to attend one in the synagogue. There are also baby namings for baby girls, bar or bat mitzvah ceremonies, Jewish weddings, and Jewish funerals. Bar or bat mitzvah ceremonies are likely the easiest to attend, and you can frequently pick up a new kippah!

Outside Book Learning

A good source of information and supplemental education are Jewish books. Even if the books are fiction, they can share valuable insights into Jewish culture, history, tradition, etc. Your rabbi might have specific books in mind to help guide you on your journey.

Some batei din require prospective Jews by Choice to keep a journal listing every book they read on Jewish life. Other batei din do not know or wish to know the list until the conversion date, and even then they still might not read it. Very early on, I was told (since I was known to have read so much over so many years) to stop reading. Given Judaism has an emphasis on studying, I actually asked the rabbis if they were sure they were Jewish!

Jewish Movies

There are lots of Jewish movies out there. I mean lots. If you are lucky, there will even be a Jewish-themed film festival near you, which can help you meet some of the cultural-event requirements while you watch movies. As with books, even fiction movies can teach you a lot about the culture that you are joining.

Other Jewish Sources

There are also book chapters, podcasts, articles, essays, blogs, radio shows, and theses are available for you to watch, read, or listen to. If you need to know it, there is surely a resource for you!

DEVELOPING A JEWISH IDENTITY

For many, the process of conversion involves developing a Jewish identity. After all, how can one be Jewish but not identify as a Jew? Development of identity can occur gradually or spontaneously. As no two people are the same, no two people will develop the same identity in the same way. With this in mind, there are a number of things that could help solidify or further a Jewish identity.

One thing I consider important is living in a Jewish area, even if you are not part of the community. Even if you live for only a short time in the area, just living in a Jewish area and moving to a mostly Gentile area might give a bit of culture shock. It was living in Miami and then moving to suburban and then rural Georgia that made me realize how very Jewish I was.

The further away from other Jews I became, the more noticeable it became. This had everything to do with the years I spent in a Jewish community. For a long time, I thought it was Floridian culture I was missing instead of Jewish culture. If I had not grown up where I did, I would not have a basic level of Jewish identity that I eventually grew into.

I would also recommend wearing Jewish-themed jewelry. Make an effort to find something that you really enjoy wearing and wear it often and proudly as a sign of your faith. Even if you do not have a strong Jewish identity to start off with, eventually you are going to find a very strong connection to your jewelry. I generally alternate between a few Star of David necklaces and a mezuzah necklace. Even if they are not visible and are hidden under your shirt, as mine frequently are, they can serve as a constant reminder for you.

Of course, even if you are not living in a highly Jewish area, just being around other Jews is going to help. Going to synagogue can provide you with a sense of community, although if you do not like going to synagogue services then perhaps it might not be the best way to help develop an identity. However, there are Jewish events such as book festivals, music festivals, and film festivals all specific to Jewish culture and heritage. There might be a listserv in your area that provides information about these events.

Jews have an obligation to make the world a better place. Simply volunteering your time and energy to social causes, almost any social cause, can remind you of what it is to be Jewish. Jews have a long history of helping the orphan, widow, and stranger in particular, as it is a biblical mandate. Additionally, the sick always need people to visit and to care for them. To do so is not only a very Jewish thing to do, it is also a mitzvah! You could also be involved with or volunteer in a Jewish non-profit organization.

Another aspect would be to take on Jewish spiritual practices, such as prayers, affixing a mezuzah on your door, and/or keeping kashrut. One rabbi suggested even doing a daily list of gratitude, which could include return of consciousness upon waking and being thankful for your soul, intelligence, individual gifts, and talents. Another prayer could be the Shema, which is normally said at least twice a day.

I try to remember to do the Shema before going to sleep, which can be difficult because I am the type to work to total exhaustion. I do however keep kosher and I have found that simply admitting that one does not eat pork will have Gentiles and other Jews making an assumption you are Jewish. I stopped eating pork and shellfish long before conversion then split milk and meat and started doing a seventy-two-minute wait time a few months before conversion. Affixing a mezuzah on your doorpost can also be a prominent symbol of Jewish identity, as it is a marker of a Jewish home, plus is also a biblical mandate.

Participating in holiday celebrations with other Jews might help keep you in touch with the Jewish community. I am not big on community events, but one of the best nights I had was at a Pesach Seder, where I had a lot of fun talking with a local Jew-lebrity (Jewish celebrity). Later, another local Jew-lebrity told me that I passed so beautifully as a Jew (there were both Jews and Gentiles at the seder) that if I had not told anyone that I was not Jewish yet no one would have known.

The next Seder, I was with another friend, and the Seder were almost all Gentiles. Twenty-five people and only two and a half Jews (the half Jew was me, who was still studying). I felt very awkward amongst the Gentiles, as I had to defend Jewish practices and explain Jewish customs. Being required to defend Jewish customs also added to my sense of having a Jewish identity, as I was being looked to as a Jew despite not being one.

Even if you are not celebrating Shabbat communally, simply lighting candles, doing Kiddush over wine or grape juice, and doing HaMotzi over challah can provide a sense of identity. Celebrating Shabbat in any way, shape, or form and thinking about it will remind you that Shabbat is ours as Jews and ours alone.

Some have suggested working with a Jew by Choice mentor or joining a support group for Jews by Choice either online or in person. I personally have not found this useful, as I had a well-developed identity and studied for years with born Jews. However, I have been placed in a position where I have had to help explain and guide other potential Jews by Choice, even ones who have been trying to convert for longer than I have been alive!

You could also spend time with a Jewish family and see if they will help teach you to live a Jewish life or teach you skills you might need to know. I have been given matzah ball soup recipes, despite the fact I do not make it (apparently my matzah balls are too large). You may also be taught how to make challah, which is something I learned on my own and now try to teach other people. My experience learning skills includes having a Conservadox Jewish woman try to teach me how to properly put on a large full-size tallit.

A very significant thing in the development of Jewish identity is to try to visit Israel. You of course do not need to do this prior to conversion. In fact, I did not go to Israel until I had already been Jewish for over a year. My identity was already pretty stable as a Jew, although it solidified my identification as a more traditionally-minded Jew. When it came time for me to leave, I cried while I waited for the airport shuttle. Everyone I know who has been to Israel has made it clear that they want to go back.

For those who cannot afford a trip to Israel, there is always the alternative of continuing to learn about Jewish topics. With the mysteries of the Torah and literally thousands of pages of Talmud, it could take a lifetime to learn all of the material. Continuing to learn Jewish topics is an excellent way to further your own identity even after conversion. Between synagogues, local Jewish community centers, other organizations, plus the internet, there is likely always a class of Jewish interest coming up soon. Take a course on Israeli dancing or Hebrew or Yiddish or Talmud Torah. Continue to learn what it means to be Jewish!

As you fall in love with your Jewish identity, apparently it can get on the nerves of some individuals. As one Jewish friend of mine said, all he read on my Facebook page for a year was how happy I was to finally be Jewish and how much I wanted to go to Israel. What he ended up learning was only a small amount of Jewish postings went to my main friend's list and there were even people on my Facebook list who knew I liked Jewish people but did not know I was Jewish.

Deciding Which Mitzvot to Follow (for the Liberal Movements)

The more liberal the movement, the more likely it is that you will have more leeway in which mitzvot you wish to fulfill. In the more traditional movements, Orthodox considers all 613 mitzvot binding and must be fulfilled if the individual mitzvah applies to you. The Conservative movement considers mitzvot binding but has some leeway in how they are interpreted.

The other movements do not consider the mitzvot binding. If you convert with one of the more liberal movements, this can either be very easy, as you can say you do not wish to follow any, or very difficult, since one can analyze each individual mitzvah and make a decision. Here are things to consider when one is deciding which mitzvot to follow.

Not Knowing How to Perform the Mitzvah

While some of the mitzvot are very straightforward and easy (i.e. not to stand by idly when a human life is in danger), others may be a bit more of a challenge. If you are unsure of how to perform a mitzvah, there will always be people who you can go to for assistance. For example, I was unsure about how to wear a full-sized tallit as it is much larger than I am, but I had someone attempt to help. Apparently given the size, no wonder I had difficulty. I needed to purchase some clips, and even then it still slips! Tefillin, one of the greatest mysteries, I am now reasonably proficient in.

Time

Being Jewish can be incredibly time consuming. A Jew is supposed to say 100 blessings each day, and men are supposed to pray three times each day. Many Americans are already overworked and overstressed. Finding the time to perform all the needed mitzvot is challenging, and for those of us who were not raised in an Orthodox household, it could be a challenge to simply remember the blessings and prayers, much less find the time to do all of them. Shabbat, in my experience, takes a lot of time to prepare for if you attempt to be shomer Shabbat.

Safety

One of the great things about Judaism is its emphasis on safety. If something is going to cause a problem, such as endangering someone's life, saving the life takes priority. If there is a mitzvah you might find difficult to do because of a safety reason, there is a good chance you will be exempt from partially or fully performing the mitzvah. Diabetics (or people who are otherwise ill) may not fast on Yom Kippur for these reasons.

Further, when I drawn to wearing tzitzit, but was worried that it might jeopardize my safety as I live in a less-than-friendly environment. I read a ruling that stated some Orthodox rabbis do not emphasize the requirement to wear visible tzitzit when a Jew is in a location known to be hostile to Jews. In this case, the tzitzit may be worn but hidden inside one's clothing.

Ethical Issues

Although Judaism focuses a lot on ethical issues, there might be some that you disagree with. For example, there are several mitzvot regarding dealing with idol worshippers, including one that involves killing witches. As I have many friends who are pagan and Wiccan, I can say my idol-worshiping friends are going to stay alive!

Finances

Sometimes things simply come down to finances. Judaism can be expensive, especially if one is giving 10% of one's income to charity. The ritual items are expensive, because people are willing to pay the money, and sometimes one has to shop around for a good deal in order to perform a mitzvah, if the mitzvah requires an item. There is a suggested list of ritual items in the appendix.

Customs

If a certain mitzvah is not commonly practiced in your community, it could make performance of the mitzvah a challenge if you are someone who can be easily influenced by peer pressure. Actually influencing others to not perform positive mitzvah is actually a negative mitzvah!

What Feels Right

There are some mitzvot that for whatever reason may simply not feel right for you. If you have such a severe objection to a mitzvah, then avoid the performance of the mitzvah and concentrate your efforts on performing mitzvot that are easier to fulfill. Perhaps down the road, more mitzvot will find their way into your ritual practice.

For me, most of my decisions are made with financial and time constraints in mind or even relate to doing the blessing prior to the performance of the mitzvah. Every mitzvah has a blessing that is to be said prior to the performance of the mitzvah.

Given I am embarrassed regarding my Hebrew skills, I would prefer to master the blessing before the performance of the mitzvah. Every question I asked regarding the mitzvah involved the question, "Can I afford to fulfill this mitzvah and do so properly?" For those I cannot do properly at the time, I work on being able to perform them in the future while I spend most of my time mastering ones that are easier to master.

Choosing Minhagim (Customs) to Follow

Part of adopting a Jewish lifestyle, you will almost certainly be expected to adopt different customs. These frequently relate to how to perform mitzvot. Different communities and even different families might have drastically different minhagim. Part of this relates to ethnicity, such as if the family are Ashkenazim or Sephardim or one of the other ethnicities.

Since the Sephardic communities tend to have fewer conversions, you will most likely be converting with an Ashkenazi rabbi and thus should likely consider yourself Ashkenazi at least to start. That being said, there are many who choose to take on Sephardic customs after conversion. As a Jew by Choice, you will likely have a variety of minhagim to choose from in comparison to born Jews, who for the most part carry generational minhagim.

There is also an opinion that additional minhagim should not be taken on, because once you perform them it is impossible to change. Since choosing which customs to follow can be a difficult decision, here are some suggestions to guide you.

Choosing the First One You Read About, Hear of, or Learn

This is the easiest method. After all, if you practice one set of customs for long enough before learning a different one, it might be easier to keep doing what you have been doing!

Choosing the Predominant Community Minhag

Depending on where you are, this might be easier said than done, as there might not be a predominant community minhag. This is particularly true in "melting pots" like the United States. If one converted in an "Old World" country, there was not as much diversity in how customs were practiced.

However, if your community does have a custom that the majority follow, you might be encouraged to adopt it in order to speed community integration. Given Ashkenazi Jews are the most common ethnic group, there is a high likelihood that your community will be following some form of Ashkenazi customs.

Choosing Your Rabbi's Minhag

The positive thing about this option is if you have any questions about the performance of a certain minhag, there is someone to ask. However, if your rabbi has customs different from Jews in other areas, if you transfer to another community, your practice might be considered unusual. Alternatively, instead of practicing your rabbi's minhag, you could choose the practices of those that turned you on to Judaism.

Choosing a Significant Other's Minhag

If your significant other is Jewish and you are converting for marriage, it might be easiest to adopt your spouse's family's customs. In fact, it is tradition in many Jewish areas for a wife to adopt the customs of her husband's family. However, if it is the husband who is the convert, it is more common for the husband to look toward the wife's family, since the husband has none of his own. All of this being said, one should not feel that marriage will lock you into a set of customs, as it is becoming more common to blend customs or to adopt or create new customs. However, by choosing a significant other's customs or creating new ones, this could certainly make one's home life easier!

Convenience

While it is probably not the best choice, some people simply pick a minhag for the convenience. For example, it is easier to wait three hours between milk and meat rather than six hours. It would be even easier to follow the Dutch custom of only waiting an hour. The most important thing is being consistent.

Investigate Family Heritage

Traditionally, the minhagim, and any tribal affiliations, would be passed through the father's side. However, if only the mother is Jewish, it would generally be her father's customs that are followed. But what happens for a Jew by Choice?

This might be harder for Jews by Choice unless they have relatives who were Jewish, as they might not be able to connect themselves to specific customs. For those who do not have known Jewish relatives, investigating one's family history is a great way to start. It can show your family that, although you converted to a new religion and adopted a new culture, your personal family history is still important to you. The Dutch custom of waiting only an hour between eating milk and meat was specifically a nod to my maternal grandmother who was Dutch, from what is now Suriname, but was of Jewish descent.

Choose Which Minhagim Are Meaningful to You

This is one of my favorite suggestions, especially for Jews by Choice who are coming into a new culture and a new religion. Obviously, Judaism is meaningful enough that conversion is or was an option. Why would there not be a choice to continue to make Judaism meaningful by any way necessary?

There is no rule stating you cannot add to your customs if you find something particularly meaningful to you later. For example, I find it very meaningful to place an orange on the Passover seder plate to represent all marginalized Jews, particularly the LGBT community. This was started in the early 1980s by Susannah Heschel.

How I Made My Choice of Minhagim

I made my choice of customs in a variety of ways. I grew up in a Jewish area, and certainly picked up a few customs that likely incorporated themselves into my daily life. Further, I dated a few observant Jews in my life as well so likely picked up additional ones from them.

In my current location, there are few Jews, and it is difficult enough to be the "lone Jew." However, when I investigated conversion again, I knew I had the option of leaving Ashkenazi tradition and following Sephardic tradition or to take on no minhagim at all.

I also knew it was important to be connected with my family history even if individual family members were not happy about my life. I looked at my family's ethnic background. Two grandparents are Italian (one from each parent), one was from Austria, and the other was indirectly from Holland (her family lived in Suriname for generations).

I knew there were Italian Jews who had their own minhagim, however I could not find anything about them. With Austria being Ashkenazi Jews and Holland having a mixture (mostly Ashkenazi with an influx of Sephardic Jews after their expulsion from Spain), I had that connection already. Plus given my insane love of the Yiddish language and food traditionally associated with Ashkenazi culture, I figured staying Ashkenazi was probably easier.

However, there were a few things that gave me pause. Hebrew is pronounced differently if you are Ashkenazi versus Sephardi, and the Ashkenazi pronunciation tends to grate on my nerves. I was not ok with committing until I learned that many Ashkenazi shuls have adopted Sephardi pronunciation.

This only left Ashkenazi dietary rules for Passover, which are much harder to deal with than Sephardi Passover rules! I decided it was worth being Ashkenazi, although I doubt my decision every Passover when I am suffering withdrawal from high-fructose corn syrup!

One minhag I have that is a little on the unusual side relates to the waiting period between meat and milk. I have a severe attention span problem, so asking me to wait three or six hours is just asking me to mess up. That being said, there is a little-known custom by Dutch Jews which requires a seventy-two minute waiting period, although anywhere from sixty minutes to ninety minutes appears to be acceptable.

I was never so happy in my life to realize that I could incorporate it into my practice while honoring my mother's side of the family. It was also the deciding factor in me taking that next leap to rabbinical kosher from biblical kosher, since it is much easier for me to wait an hour than it is for me to remember when the last time I ate meat was!

Choosing a Hebrew Name

Every Jew is supposed to have a Hebrew name, and before your conversion your rabbi will want to know what the name you chose is. This name will be written on your Shtar Giur (certificate of conversion), and there will be a naming ceremony after the mikvah where you are officially given your new name as a Jew.

This is your legal Jewish name and is the name that is used on all official Jewish documentation. This is the name you will be called up to the Torah by, the name you will be married under, and this will be the name used if, G-d forbid, you should ever need prayers said on your behalf. While you can take as long as you need to pick your Hebrew name, I consider it fundamental to developing a Jewish identity, so I recommend thinking about this early.

A Hebrew name is divided into three components. For example, my Hebrew name is Mordechai Yisrael ben Avraham Avinu v'Sarah Imanu. The first component is your personal Hebrew name. Even if it is several words, it is simply treated as one name. While I will simply respond to Mordechai, technically Mordechai Yisrael is my first name. The second component refers to the gender of the person and whether they are a son of (ben) or a daughter of (bat or bas) their parents. The third component is a patronymic and/or matronymic component identifying the parents of the offspring with the patronymic referring to the father and the matronymic referring to the mother. The traditional naming convention for a Jew by Choice for the third component is Avraham Avinu v'Sarah Imanu, which translates to Abraham Our Father and Sarah Our Mother, symbolizing that while the new Jew does not have biological Jewish parents, they still have a set of spiritual parents, Abraham and Sarah.

There are a few Jews by Choice who are able to convince their beit din to allow them to take on a different patronymic last name. This can allow the Jew by Choice to hide their status more easily and not have their status as Jews questioned in the future. This was more common during times when conversion to Judaism was a death sentence. I know two Jews by Choice who do not have the traditional patronymic name. Since I can often pass as a born Jew, I begged to be given a different patronymic like the other friends I had. Unfortunately, I was not granted that indulgence, but I have grown to like the patronymic, although I am still likely to not add Avinu or Imanu depending on where I am and how well I am passing.

Unlike Jews by birth, Jews by Choice have the ability to choose their own Hebrew first names. While it is generally in Hebrew, there are cases when the "Hebrew" name is actually Yiddish or Aramaic. However, since there is a complicated set of rules regarding what happens if the Hebrew name is partially in Yiddish, I am going to make the assumption that your Hebrew name will be Hebrew and your rabbi will be able to help arrange your name properly if you want Yiddish in your Hebrew name.

Despite the fact you will receive your Hebrew name officially at the ceremony, you can start thinking about your name long before you meet with a rabbi. There are several ways to choose your name, although some communities, mostly Orthodox, may not allow you to have an extensive choice.

Books

When I was originally searching for my name, I started off by reading books. I started to work through Teluskin's "Jewish Literacy" book, and as I was reading the entries I was recording names I liked the sound of or I liked the story behind. Of course, if you do not wish to read roughly eight hundred or so pages, you could pick up a baby name book or a book that specializes in Jewish/Hebrew names. On the internet, there are several websites you can go to in order to find Hebrew-specific names. Additionally, if your Hebrew is good enough, you could pick up a Hebrew dictionary and glance through it.

Inspiration

If you're lucky, your Hebrew name will strike you like part of mine struck me. Always listen to your gut if you feel a name is calling to you. I had just decided that I needed to start looking at Hebrew names when my name hit me. I was only a few dozen pages into Jewish Literacy and had only five names or so on my list when I was getting tired. Not a surprise there, I had a lot of pages left to cover.

However, I closed my book and stood up to go make myself some lunch. I barely stood up from my bed before my brain decided to sing to me five lines from a song that felt so familiar, but I couldn't place it. I knew the lines were somewhere in the middle of the song, but I was more amazed that I recognized it vaguely as a song from my past. The most important aspect of the song, and likely the reason why it was being sung, was because it was about someone naming their young boy after someone else's Uncle Mordechai. Mordechai being an important character in the Book of Esther.

After hearing this earworm for four hours, which was more than one really needed to hear five lines of a song, I looked up toward the Heavens and asked if this was a sign that I was supposed to consider Mordechai as a possible name for myself. The song seemed to become louder.

I agreed to write it down on the possible names list if the song could PLEASE go away, because four hours was four hours too long! I wrote Mordechai down, and the song went away immediately. I looked up the song lyrics that had so annoyed me.

The lyrics were part of Tevye's Dream from "Fiddler on the Roof," a movie I had not seen in well over a decade. That night, I had a dream where someone kept trying to get my attention by calling Mordechai. Finally, in the dream I turned around and said "WHAT?" When I woke up the next morning, I knew my search was over. I was Mordechai.

As I learned later, there was no way I could have avoided the name Mordechai. There were too many things in Mordechai's favor, not the least of which because I love Purim. As a matter of fact, my father wanted to name me Mork as a baby after the TV show "Mork & Mindy," his favorite show. As it turns out, Mork is short for Mordechai.

Biblical Character or Location you Like

The Jewish Bible is full of interesting characters and locations. Are there any Biblical locations you like? My mother wanted my secular name to be Jordan, which would have potentially been an acceptable Hebrew name. Is there a particular story that resonates with you or a particular character you would like to have more qualities of?

Perhaps you wish to have the leadership qualities of Moshe (Moses) or his siblings Aaron or Miriam? Lot was a righteous man, the only one in Sodom. Perhaps you would rather be more traditional and stick with one of the names of the Patriarchs or Matriarchs? In some communities, you might only have this option. Personally, one of my favorite characters is Isaac, and I really wanted to squeeze his name into my Hebrew name, but that wasn't meant to be.

Holiday

Are there any particular Jewish holidays you feel drawn to or that your conversion date is near? Lovers of Purim might be drawn to Mordechai or Esther, for example. Lovers of Shavuot might prefer Ruth, Naomi, or Boaz.

English Names into Hebrew

You also have the ability to convert an English name into Hebrew. You could take your secular name and find Hebrew names with similar underlying meanings. There are websites that make this easier. Another possibility would be to take a relative's name and turn it into a Hebrew name for yourself. Remember, Ashkenazi tradition states the relative should be deceased. In Sephardic tradition, the relative can be alive.

Getting Advice From Others

Sometimes, it is best to simply ask for advice from people who know you well and are familiar with Judaism. When I had a list of possible "double decker" names, I asked my friends (on Facebook) which of the five options they liked the most, since I did not have a strong preference. More than a few offered new names.

I told them I really did not want to add more options and instead wanted to reduce the list. One of my beit din members decided to give his opinion. Knowing my struggle as well as he did and knowing how much I have fought to be recognized as Jewish, he made a very compelling argument for me to take on either Yaakov (Jacob) or Yisrael (Israel). Jacob wrestled with a man (or an angel depending who is telling the story) and was renamed Israel, which means, "One who wrestles with G-d." As soon as I wrote Mordechai Yisrael on a sheet of paper, I was certain it was my name.

THE CONVERSION CEREMONY

Nothing worried me more than the conversion itself. If you ask any of my beit din members, they will tell you if you looked up "stereotypical neurotic Jew" in the dictionary, a photo of me during the few weeks prior to my conversion would be next to the definition. I was nervous. I was terrified. Suddenly something I worked so hard to get was going to be given to me! I was finally going to be Jewish!

I was excited enough to have a countdown on my computer counting down the seconds until the ceremony was to begin. However, every time I looked at the countdown, I panicked. As the seconds ticked away, I was that much closer to being an adult Jewish man bound by all 613 mitzvot! It didn't matter that half of the rules are suspended since we no longer have a Temple in Jerusalem. I still panicked and nothing could calm me down.

Really though, it was probably less the 613 mitzvot that drove me to panic and more that no matter what there were still things I did not experience and educational experiences I would never have. I did not get the benefit of going to Hebrew school or Jewish summer camp. I did not get the benefit of going to synagogue regularly or watching my father put on a tallit or tefillin, and suddenly I was going to be obliged to do it on my own. There was no longer a play period.

There was no longer an excuse of, "Okay, I did not do this perfectly, but I am a Gentile, so it's okay since G-d does not command me to do so," or "I did not do this at all, but that is ok because I am a Gentile." Instead, if I missed something or did something wrong, with the same action I went from being an extraordinarily righteous Gentile to being a sinning Jew. That made me nervous.

Though I knew I was more academically knowledgeable than many Jews by birth, I still knew I was behind in some areas and felt like an imposer in comparison to those born Jewish. I felt very behind for a Jew and did not want to feel like I was constantly playing catch-up. From what I have learned, however, this impostor-like feeling is completely normal. Almost no one feels fully prepared and knowledgeable in all areas of Judaic Studies before one converts to Judaism.

Another issue I knew nothing of had to do with what was going to occur in most of the ceremony, and despite the entire beit din saying the meeting with me was just a formality I knew it wasn't. It was an interview, and I do poorly in interview settings even if my friends are the ones doing the interviewing! I also do not like going into things blind or getting surprises. I felt like I had to prepare well for the lifecycle event, but no one told me what to do.

Choosing Your Conversion Date

There is a possibility you will not have a lot of choice when you convert due to the beit din members' schedules and when the mikvah is available. Additionally, conversions must occur on a weekday and before sundown. Shabbat, along with many other Jewish holidays, are off-limits because status changes cannot occur on Shabbat. One rabbi asked me to come up with a list of dates (birthdays, anniversaries, etc) that played a part in my life. He wanted me to be sure I would remember the day. When I came up with the list, we compared his schedule and mine, and our schedules could not match up, except on my birthday, which I did not want to convert on, because it was during the Three Weeks, the saddest part of the Jewish year.

While that rabbi did not pan out, my final rabbi randomly selected my birthday at my birth time. He did not know this when he selected the date and time. While I still had my reservations, I decided it was a sign that maybe it would be safe to convert during the Three Weeks, especially since the secular date (not the Hebrew date) had lucky number eighteen in it. Eighteen symbolizes "life" so would be a good time to convert secularly.

My mikvah attendant was worried when she realized I was converting during the Three Weeks and, like myself, was almost in a panic once everyone started singing "Siman Tov" near the end of the ceremony, as singing is forbidden by more traditional movements during this time period.

There are other issues that might play a factor in choosing your conversion date. If you are male and need to be circumcised, you should wait until after you are healed before you immerse in the mikvah. This is not only to eliminate potential health risks, such as an infection, but also because you cannot wear anything (such as a bandage) that would be a barrier between you and the mikvah water. If you are female, some rabbis will not allow a conversion to take place when one is menstruating. So if this is a concern, you might want to ask your rabbi what would happen in the case of surprise bleeding.

How to Write the Conversion Essay

Many rabbis require an essay... a spiritual autobiography as it were. Part of the purpose of this is to introduce you and your journey to the beit din. All paths to Judaism are different and personal, although the destinations are similar and the beit din wants to know your story and learn about YOU. For some beit din members, this could be their only prior contact with you before the conversion.

I was given no guidelines initially. I was, however, writing my conversion story for a book chapter that was to be published, which spoke about my journey toward Judaism. If there was one thing being in graduate school taught me, it was to try to find ways to make your papers count multiple times when possible.

So as I was writing my story, I decided it would be the very first draft of my conversion essay and would have to suffice until I received further instruction. It ended up being fourteen pages double spaced, and I knew the odds were low that anyone would want to read it! Once I told a beit din member about the draft and described it, only then did

I receive feedback. I was told no more than seven pages double spaced. The essay should cover several points, including:

1. What brings you to Judaism?
2. What challenges have you faced in regards to exploring/practicing Judaism?
3. What are some highlights of your journey? Were there any low points?
4. What are your favorite holidays and rituals?
5. After conversion, what is next for you?

The first three questions are important ones because they help the beit din learn about your background and history. The fourth forces you to think about what rituals you have been involved with and why those things are important to you. I also believe this gives an insight into your personality.

After all, someone whose favorite holiday is the fun-filled holiday of Purim might be very different from someone who would prefer the more serious holiday of Yom Kippur! The last question is also an important one.

Upon conversion, you join a new community and a new culture, and the beit din has to be sure you are going to have a Jewish future. Your rabbi might guide you with different questions to answer. One of my friends was given ten questions, and she started off each answer with a haiku. Most of the questions she was given involved the questions I listed.

In my first draft, I already mentioned what brought me to Judaism and some of the challenges I faced. Even some of the highlights and low points were already mentioned in much more depth than most would want. I answered the rest and eventually shrunk the word count.

I found thinking about the holidays and the rituals to be difficult. It was something I never really considered. I decided on three favorite holidays (Purim, Tu B'Shevat, and Shabbat) and mentioned why each was important. Rituals, I also had to think about. Some ritualistic practices had become such a part of me over much of the past two decades that not only did I have to think about what was considered a ritual, I had to think whether or not they were Jewish in origin!

Thinking about what was next was also difficult. I had no doubt I was going to have a Jewish future. Why would my future be all that much different from my past? I knew I wanted to learn my beloved Yiddish. Few things soothe me as being sung to or spoken to in Yiddish, even if my comprehension is not there.

I knew I was going to have to study Hebrew. I knew I wanted to visit Israel, which was a long-term dream of mine. What else was there for me to do? I did not have what I felt they were looking for... namely the community connection. Luckily, during the several drafts I had to go through for my rabbi, a surprise volunteer position with a Jewish non-profit popped up, and I slipped it right in!

I went through four or five more drafts of the essay before my sponsoring rabbi would approve it. A version of my conversion essay is located in the appendix as a sample. With the exception of removing names for privacy and eliminating a reference to a community that turned out to be a disastrous association, it is exactly how it was submitted to the beit din.

Preparing for the Brit Milah (If Needed)

For uncircumcised men, a circumcision (brit milah) will need to be arranged, unless there are medical reasons why one could not be performed. For circumcised men, a ritual drop of blood (a hatafat dam brit) is required. In the hatafat dam brit, an area near where the foreskin would attach is cleaned using alcohol, and then a drop of blood is extracted, such as with a sharp sterile razor, a sterile pin, a sterile lancet, or sterile needle. The blood is collected on a gauze pad and shown to witnesses. This is harmless with no real chance of complications, although many men are terrified of the event itself.

A full brit milah is more complicated. The average mohel, ritual circumciser, has very little experience circumcising adults. Adult circumcision might require licensed doctors, expert mohelim, post-surgery care, although it is usually done in an out-patient environment. Generally those who perform these surgeries are either urologists or general surgeons.

The Reform and Conservative movements have been training and certifying physicians and surgeons as mohelim. If a surgeon is not a certified mohel but the surgeon is Jewish, the mohel is unnecessary because any Jew can perform the blessings. If the surgeon is not Jewish, a mohel or any other Jew should be present in the operating room or surgical suite in order to recite the blessings.

An adult circumcision is a short, thirty-minute or so procedure to perform. Depending on the patient, preparing for the anesthesia could take longer. Many patients are able to return to work the next day with a prescription for a mild painkiller.

Although dissolvable sutures are often used, the surgeon will usually wish to check the healing process periodically, and he or she will likely provide the patient with post-operative instructions. Complications are rare.

Preparing for the Beit Din

Nothing could have scared me more than the beit din. Apparently, this is not unusual. Every Jew by Choice I have asked (except for one who had a very sketchy conversion) has said they were the most nervous about the beit din.

In theory, no prospective Jew fails the beit din. The head of your beit din, usually your sponsoring rabbi, is not supposed to arrange a meeting with the rest of the members until he or she believes you can pass.

This sometimes makes people feel better to know this, but then others might feel even worse as some may feel they are lying about their knowledge or feel like they are really impostors. Now people do fail, but generally, you have to say something so against a fundamental core Jewish belief that they must fail you. For example, unless you are converting Messianic ("Jews for Jesus"), admitting you believe in Jesus as the son of G-d could potentially be a problem!

Even though batei din do not generally fail someone, depending on the movement, the conversion might be delayed. I have heard of Conservative and Orthodox Jews by Choice who had their beit din meeting but the beit din learned there was a hole in the potential convert's knowledge so drastic that the final conversion needed to be delayed until the hole was rectified.

This was probably the thing I feared the most. I had friends waiting outside the library where I was having my beit din meeting. One prepared a huge celebratory lunch for me. Last thing I wanted was to walk out and tell my friends that I spent years studying but was still not allowed to convert yet because I missed something!

I did not know what questions to expect or how to prepare other than to do what several Conservative and Orthodox rabbis recommended for their students. The primary recommendation was to record in detail the conversion curriculum, what Jewish books you read, what Jewish movies you watched, any Jewish podcasts you listened to, etc., and periodically update the beit din and have them recommend more educational materials.

As someone whose sponsoring rabbi claimed he was going to give me supplemental material once I completed my introduction to Judaism class and then did not, I was hoping the remaining members of the beit din would look over the lists I provided and tell me if there were any holes.

Of course, I wanted this guidance because I know myself and, like most people, would prefer to study things I enjoy and avoid things I hate. Was Hebrew underrepresented? Was Kabbalah overrepresented? What about the rest of the subjects? As an over-neurotic almost-Jew, I even cared about the proportion of books to movies per subject. Did I watch too many Holocaust movies and not read enough Holocaust books? For the record, I found it easier to watch the movies than read the books, as I could leave the room if I had to. Not as easy to do that with a book. Plus with my subscriptions to on-demand streaming services, all they seemed to have were Holocaust movies under their Jewish section!

No one told me how I was doing curriculum wise. I begged. I pleaded. Finally, I gave up. The Shabbat before my conversion date, I refused to do anything but relax. Previously, I would have spent the time studying or reading. My time on Shabbat was primarily a date with HaShem, so it felt awkward for me to purposefully be avoiding anything Jewish related. I knew if I studied, I was going to get myself worked because I knew I could not learn enough about Judaism before then. I did not need more stress. I do not remember if I even streamed any services, but I certainly know I did not read any books.

I do not, as a general rule, like interviews unless I am in complete control. I can fail an interview like nobody's business. Knowing there was going to be a fifteen to twenty minute interview with three rabbis to decide whether I could officially join their people terrified me. This was my graduate thesis defense all over again, except this time I knew there was no way I could trick them if they asked a question I did not know.

The only thing that kept me from calling things off due to my fear of the beit din interview was when a few Orthodox Jews by Choice told me the most they were going to do was insure I knew basic things about Judaism such as what Yom Kippur is. I have my holidays down, so I was not worried about that.

So I was fairly certain that when two of my beit din members said they were going to ask me the names of all the kings of Israel, in order, it was probably a joke, although at least that would have been something I could memorize! Other Jews by Choice told me the beit din was a set of open-ended questions. Another person, a rabbinical student who was also a Jew by Choice, told me it was more like people "just wanting to hang out with you for a few minutes." With my social issues at the time, no one would have wanted to hang out with me for a few minutes!

The night before my conversion, I only slept three hours. It was not intentional; it was due to a sprained ankle and having to wake up at 4:30 am to pick up my mikvah attendant (and her husband) who lived a few hours away, as their car broke down a few days prior. I was not in the most coherent of moods. I would recommend sleeping more on your conversion day. If I had a full night's sleep and was not responsible for a few other lives in my car, I would have brought anti-anxiety medication with me to take before the meeting as the meeting was that stressful.

When I walked into the synagogue housing the mikvah, the first person I saw was a reverend friend of mine who wanted to come to a Jewish conversion. The second was my sponsoring rabbi.

Apparently, one of my other beit din members was already there. Not long later, several of my friends showed up. As I waited for my last beit din member to arrive, I was shown the mikvah again (which I had already seen on a previous occasion), then when another prospective Jew by Choice arrived I gave her a tour as well.

Even though I remember speaking to all my friends and talking to the two rabbis before me, my brain and heart were crying out and talking to someone else. If someone had a microphone in my head, they would have heard my brain cry, "Please G-d, please G-d, please let me pass," interspersed with blessings that were half in Hebrew and half in English.

One of the crazier things was "Baruch atah Adonai Eloheinu Melech ha'olam, please let them see what You do and let me come home!" My brain was periodically reciting the Shema as if I was entering a life threatening situation.

As my last beit din member arrived and we entered the library, it was show time. As I gave them the things I had for them (and slid my list of books/movies/classes to one of them), I quickly thought about how I knew each of them.

One rabbi was newly ordained and was officially only considered a "rabbinical fellow" locally, as he did not attend a traditional school. Of everyone present at the entire conversion, I knew him the longest... about ten months. (Technically, I had spoken once prior to the reverend friend a year prior, but we did not become friends until more recently.)

This rabbi taught the most recent conversion course I took, and I was currently taking another course with him. I also volunteered with his non-profit. He knew my struggles and, as he identifies as a Kabbalist, I felt very comfortable telling him some of the weirder experiences which brought me back to Judaism. He also met my partner and met my step-daughter. I do not know exactly what I was expecting from him.

The next rabbi was the youngest of the three, only a few years older than I was. I first met him only two weeks prior to the conversion, not long after I learned who my third member was. Since I was freaking out, I arranged a meeting with him so I could at least see this mysterious third member.

He was a very nice guy, one of the nicest people I've met in my entire life, and calmed many of my fears while telling me stories of others he converted who did not have the Jewish background that I did. Since I was worried about Hebrew pronunciation, he told me a wonderful story about a woman who would call a yarmulke by the name of Yamaha, which is a vehicle, not a hat.

At that pre-conversion meeting, he told me I had a lot of support from my conversion teacher and this spoke volumes about my readiness. He spent so much time dispelling my fears that several months later I declared him my favorite rabbi. I at least knew he was not going to be the hardest to convince at the official meeting. As a matter of fact, of the beit din, he was the only person who remembered to wish me a happy birthday.

My third was my sponsoring rabbi (rosh beit din), who sat at the head of the table. At this point, I'd known him about three months. I knew he did not know me as well as the rabbinical fellow, and this came out periodically in our conversations.

He was a nice guy but sometimes was a little intimidating to me, probably because my fate was in his hands. How much of being intimidated by him was simply due to my own anxiety is hard to know. I find him much less intimidating now... except when he puts his glasses way down on the end of his nose.

I barely had myself settled in the chair before the questions came. The questions did not come from my sponsoring rabbi, which is who I feared, but instead from one of the other members... namely my teacher. I more than a few times thought perhaps suggesting him was a bad idea.

After all, he knew much more than what I put in my five-page conversion essay. As soon as I saw a copy of my essay highlighted, I knew he was not going to make this easy on me. No one else had a copy of the essay or at least not where I could see it! For years, I threatened to call this chapter, "Preparing for the beit din: aka my My nudnik Kabbalist beit din member who asks too many questions."

I cannot tell you how many questions were asked or even all of the subjects covered. I know there were no questions specifically about Judaism or anything along those lines, although I vaguely remember a question about Israel... I believe it involved my threat of aliyah even though I had not visited Israel yet.

One of the first things said to me when I entered that room was a comment about the beit din not really caring about what was in one's head but instead what was in one's heart. As someone who does not speak much about feelings—I am on the autistic spectrum after all—I find it difficult to really get into details about why I needed to officially be Jewish.

There is a saying amongst autistics that "Text is Life," as most of us prefer to communicate by writing even if we are fully verbal! This combined with being scared, running on no sleep, and knowing my sponsoring rabbi made me rewrite the essay several times in order to make my full journey less mystical convinced me that making sure everyone was happy with my answers was going to be a challenge.

If I answered the full truth, the Kabbalist would know I was telling the truth, but the sponsoring rabbi might be concerned. If I answered in a way I believed the sponsoring rabbi wanted to hear, the Kabbalist would know I wasn't telling the entire truth. I was not particularly trying to evade questions, but it felt like I was needing to follow a careful line between two extremes.

I was asked about my family. My partner is not Jewish, and by allowing me to convert an interfaith family would be created. There was mention of my step-daughter, who had prior expressed interest in learning more. There was concern about my partner's dislike of Judaism, such as the concept of tzedakah.

I was warned there was a fear of difficulties with "Shalom bayit," peace in the home. All I could do was state that I have been doing my best to be a good partner without compromising myself, but I cannot control my other half. I also mentioned I did not expect anyone else to convert because I wanted to. This was my journey, not theirs. (For more information about creating an Interfaith family see Special Topics.)

I remember being asked about my class work and the things I learned in class and if there was anything particularly meaningful. It is hard to look your teacher dead in the eye and say yours was a refresher course for me. I did not say this at the beit din, but I had said this in the past.

Luckily, he also knew I was also attending an Orthodox-run internet based yeshiva that provided me access to more information than I ever really wanted to know or could have ever imagined knowing. So he targeted that. One of the courses I took was a course on the laws of conversion. One of the classes was on converting without a beit din. It was a minority opinion, but an opinion I latched onto as if it was a lifesaver and I was a drowning man. Apparently, there was a Talmudic reference that declared living as a Jew among Jews makes one Jewish whether or not a beit din officially rules. This was something I sensed a year prior when I realized HaShem considered me Jewish even if the rabbis did not. I remember looking at my hand on the table in front of me. I did not want to look up at the beit din, but I told them what I learned in yeshiva and said it really did not matter what their final ruling on my status was.

I was going to be Jewish regardless. This was the most honest answer I could give, and it was one that came from my heart. I did not even realize what I was saying until the words came out of my mouth! I do not know what they were thinking, but I am sure none of them were more surprised than I was when I realized I told the beit din their opinion did not matter to me!

After a few more questions about issues with the community and how I was going to be involved in synagogue life (see Special Topics), I was never so happy to hear all three of them agree I should be converted. I am not sure if they heard my huge sigh of relief.

The rest of the meeting with the beit din really does not require much preparation and is far from frightening. All that was required was the reading of the declaration of faith and signing of the conversion certificate. In my case, the declaration of faith was written on the conversion certificate itself, however this is not always the case.

To summarize, the declaration of faith has you state you are converting of your own free will, your loyalty is forever with the Jewish people, and an agreement to raise your children as Jews. Your conversion paperwork should be treated as a legal document because for all practical purposes it is, and you may need it again in the future.[2] You will be signing your secular name in two spots, not your Hebrew one. After all, you have not officially been given your Hebrew name. The beit din will

---

[2]   Ironically, less than one year I after acquired it, I had to use it in a secular setting to get my United States passport.

sign their secular name and their Hebrew name. While two of the beit din were signing, the sponsoring rabbi got me started in the mikvah.

Preparing for the Mikvah

After the beit din approves you, the next step is going to the mikvah, which I will discuss in a minute.

When I was preparing for my conversion, I asked several people what I needed to bring to the mikvah. Yes, I had seen what was going to be "my" mikvah a few months before my conversion, but I was too busy listening to the rabbi discuss the mikvah and looking around realizing that someday I was going to be there again, so I did not pay any attention as to what was in the preparation room. As it turned out, once I finally obtained an answer, most of the things one would need were already there. Towels were there, robes, and I saw some basic toiletries, although you might want to bring your own, just in case. Of course, it is wise to verify with your own mikvah what will be provided.

You will almost certainly have an attendant in the mikvah with you. Generally, this person will be the same sex as you are, although you might have a choice if you are transgender or intersexed. My rabbi emailed me and gave me the option. As I was emailing back to say that I really did not care, a friend of mine called me randomly and after asking who was going to be the attendant, she offered herself.

Since the mikvah attendant has to be a knowledgeable Jew who knows the rules of mikvah, she was appropriate. When I asked my rabbi if she could be the one since she offered herself and she uses mikvah periodically, he said she was fine. Your mikvah attendant will help guide you through the process.

When you first enter the mikvah area, you will likely enter a changing room or preparation room. It will likely have a toilet, sink, shower, and possibly a bathtub. There might also be pamphlets on important health-related topics and there might also be cards with the proper rituals and blessings.

In order to qualify as a proper conversion (or any proper purification as the mikvah is used for many things), nothing can come between you and the mikvah water. Similar to how some public pools recommend or require a quick shower before you enter, you should bathe prior to the mikvah.

All bandages, clothing, makeup, and jewelry must be removed before you wash and must stay off until the immersion is complete. If you have a medical device that cannot easily be removed, please consult a rabbi. Men and women, if you normally shave, then you should do so prior to immersing. The mikvah is not meant to be more than a ritual bath, so you must be clean before immersion.

The Orthodox may require a long soak in a bathtub to help loosen any dirt or loose skin that might be difficult to remove, then a shower to remove the rest of the dirt. Others might require just a shower. In the shower, you should wash your hair, face, and body to attempt to get every part of you clean.

There was already shampoo and body wash in the shower of my mikvah along with more health care pamphlets.[3] I will confess it was difficult for me to figure out how to get hot water no matter how far I turned it. If my beit din ever wondered what was taking me so long, that was a part of it! I did eventually get hot water, and there was much rejoicing.

After you wash, put on a robe and call for your attendant. Some mikvah have a phone you can use or another way to summon the attendant. Since my attendant stayed with me during the entire bathing process, which I found a little awkward, she went out to tell them I was ready.

Once you and the mikvah attendant are in the mikvah immersion room itself, the beit din will report to their location. They will most likely be standing in a room right off from the immersion room with a window high up where they can hear you but not see you. I personally did not notice their section until I saw my sponsoring rabbi close the

---

[3]   If you are wondering about the health pamphlets, many Orthodox and Conservadox women use mikvah monthly and there is a push to do monthly breast exams while preparing for mikvah. This is a smart idea which I am sure will save many lives.

door separating the preparation room. I originally thought it was just a weird design of the building (as my attendant did).

Once the beit din are in place, the mikvah attendant will have you take off the robe. You might turn around for an inspection to assure there is nothing loose such as a stray hair. A single stray hair could invalidate a conversion as the requirements state that nothing can come between the soon-to-be Jew by Choice and the mikvah water. A good attendant will take the job seriously. Right after I was considered clear for immersion, a single hair fell, and she grabbed it right off me and held it far from her. Some groups have the custom to burn a stray hair that falls.

I was then cleared again for immersion and I walked to the edge of the mikvah steps and waited for instruction. Before you enter the mikvah, your rabbi will give you final instructions and it is a good thing he did.

I was originally told by one beit din member what the instructions were going to be, but my sponsoring rabbi gave me slightly different ones. For example, I was originally told I was likely going to immerse the first time then do the first blessing. The internet agreed with this, since you are not Jewish until you submerse, thus you do not have to do a blessing before a mitzvah. Once you are Jewish, you have to do the blessing first. I was told to do the blessing first and then immerse. Do it in whichever order your rabbi wishes.

The first blessing in transliterated Hebrew, is written, "Baruch atah Adonai Eloheinu Melech ha'olam asher kidshanu b'mitzvotav v'tzivanu al hatevilah." This means, "Blessed are You, L-rd our G-d, King of the Universe, Who has sanctified us with the mitzvot and commanded us concerning immersion."

You then enter the mikvah waters and walk down the steps until you get to the bottom. You will fully immerse and pick your feet off the floor of the mikvah so that no parts of you are touching anything other than the water. A warning: depending on the mikvah, you might not want to open your eyes. I remember originally bumping along the side very briefly. I was startled and opened my eyes. This was when I learned our mikvah was heavily, heavily chlorinated!

I felt like I was dying when I came back up, coughing and choking, plus my eyes were burning. I was a little in shock (partially from the chlorination as I thought it had to be pure rainwater) and then realized I still had to go under two more times! I rested against the side of the mikvah where my mikvah attendant was standing and had placed the list of blessings so it was easier for me to read.

The next blessing, which is a very good blessing to keep memorized, was the shehecheyanu which is said at all special occasions and rare events. In transliterated Hebrew, it is written, "Baruch atah Adonai Eloheinu Melech ha'olam shehecheyanu, vekiymanu, vehigiyanu lazman hazeh." This means, "Blessed are You, L-rd our G-d, King of the Universe, Who has kept us alive and sustained us, and enabled us to reach this day."

Then another immersion, another batch of choking that hopefully you will not have, then the Shema, if required. The Shema is another good one to keep memorized. In transliterated Hebrew, it is written, "Shema Yisrael, Adonai Eloheinu, Adonai Echad." This means, "Hear O Israel, the L-rd is our G-d, the L-rd is One."

After three dunks, you are Jewish! Congratulations! Mazel tov!

Once you dry off and get dressed, you will be named.

Since I did not mention this earlier, I would really recommend having your phone completely off during the entire process. I was called by the most antisemitic member of my family (who was calling to wish me a happy birthday) right as I was getting dressed from the mikvah!

Naming Ceremony

I do not like surprises, any form of surprises. So although I was able to find almost everything relating to the conversion, one thing eluded me. The naming ceremony. My Google-fu failed me, and no conversion blog or resource talked about it. I was not the only person who did everything they could to look for an adult naming for a conversion. My mikvah attendant also tried asking around and searching on the internet and elsewhere. There simply was not much in the way of information.

I was shaking when I walked into the sanctuary, mostly because I had no idea what was going to occur. I had the presence of mind (at least) to acknowledge the mezuzah, and I probably only did that because someone who walked into the sanctuary right before me did so! I think that was my first mitzvah as a Jew.

I was asked to come up to the bima with one of the rabbis (the one I knew the least as my sponsoring rabbi had to leave for a meeting) while my friends sat in the pews.

There were several readings, some by the rabbi and at least two by me, luckily all in English. Most of the readings came from primarily the Book of Ruth, Ruth being the most famous Jew by Choice. One of the passages included Ruth's famous oath, "For wherever you go, I will go; And wherever you lodge, I will lodge; Your people shall be my people, and your G-d, my G-d." The Shema was also said.

When I thought we were almost finished, the Ark was opened, and I was hoping I was not going to be handed a Torah scroll, but I was. I am less than 5'4", and at the time weighed in the mid-120s and could barely carry a bag of groceries.

As my mikvah attendant told me later, I turned white as a sheet, and she was just hoping I would not drop it! I was thinking the same thing! I still do not know how I was able to hold and not drop the forty to fifty-pound Torah scroll. I barely remember what was said other than it was a very long reminder that while that particular scroll belongs to the shul, the Torah itself belongs to me too.

Then was the naming itself where I was given my new name.

I thought we were finished, but we were not. The next stage was something my teacher stated he had not seen before. The rabbi had everyone come up, place a hand on me (all at once so they surrounded me) and give me a blessing.

I was blessed with everything including wisdom, peace, clarity, strength, and trust.[4] After that they started singing, and while it takes

---

4   For those who were not present, but I thought well of I also asked for a blessing from them, one gave me the priestly blessing (I did not know he was qualified to give that although I would later find out that he was in fact a kohan) and another blessed me with self esteem and confidence.

much to embarrass me I will state that it was a bit embarrassing. Plus it was still during the Three Weeks of Mourning, so there should not have been any singing!

Beit Din Gifts

While it is not necessary, it has become a custom to give thank you gifts to your beit din. After all, they are doing you a favor while, some might argue, also performing a mitzvah.

For those who are converting on a budget, a simple heartfelt thank you card and message will do wonders. For those who know their beit din very well, a gift tailored to their individual interests might be very welcome. Of my beit din, I only knew one of them very well, and he was not my rosh beit din. I did not want to give him something more than I gave everyone else, so I gave everyone the same things, although different cards with different messages inside.

When I was looking for suggestions on what to give beit din members, Jewish music and Jewish books were suggested. However, since I would not know what books to purchase or what they already owned, I opted to give each of them an $18 gift card to Amazon. That way someone could purchase anything they wished. Eighteen, of course, symbolizes life, and eighteen or its multiples are frequently used in Judaism.

Someone also suggested purchasing a favorite kosher wine as a gift, particularly to your sponsoring rabbi. However, I do not drink and really do not like many wines, plus could not afford wine as it was. Instead, since I just taken up baking, I gave each of them a loaf of raisin challah I made the previous night. As challah is considered to be difficult to make, many of my friends joked my real final exam was not the beit din interview, but instead the bread I gave to them!

Tzedakah

A common tradition that often occurs after lifecycle events, such as conversion, is the ritual giving of tzedakah. Your rabbi might request or suggest you give tzedakah and might suggest a specific charity in mind. This is up to your rabbi and you entirely. Tzedakah is one of my favorite mitzvot, so I knew this was going to be part of my conversion regardless of whether or not my rabbi requested it or not.

I briefly worked with one rabbi who advised a tzedakah payment of $180 to his discretionary fund on top of all the other fees he required. The sponsoring rabbi who finally converted me did not require a tzedakah payment.

He told me I could if I wanted to, but it was by no means required. We even had a brief misunderstanding because I said that I felt it was required and was something I had to do. Some internal sense reminded me that while this might not be something I was required to do, it was something I am obligated to do as a good Jew and that this was a mitzvah that was very important to me to fulfill. I donated $90 to his discretionary fund and $18 to another charity.

There is another custom to invite the poor to parties, or at the very least donate money (generally 3% of the cost of the party) to feed the poor. While I do not know how much my friend spent on my conversion lunch, I had a rather large sack of pennies that I took to a CoinStar machine and donated all the money to a charity that feeds the impoverished. In this way, the poor participated in my party, and I believed that hopefully this would bring a bit of luck and help start my new Jewish life off on the right foot.

AFTER CONVERSION

The mikvah is only the beginning, not the end. One thinks that is it, one is a Jew, and that is it. A lot of things happen or might happen once it is over, so some things should be discussed.

Phenomena of the Disappearing Convert

Although I have not met a Jew by Choice who "disappeared" after conversion, given the amount of times this was brought up as a potential subject for me to investigate and the amount of times I have been praised for still being observant after conversion, I assume something must be occurring. I am not beyond doing research in areas that I have not seen or heard of before!

I asked some people who have heard of this phenomena to tell me more. One colleague who had tried to convert for a number of years mentioned two women in her synagogue who were allowed to convert (while my friend was not), and as soon as they converted they never attended shul again. To me, it sounded like that old joke about a rabbi giving mice a bar mitzvah to get rid of them.[5]

---

[5] Three rabbis are standing around talking when one of them says, "We've got a terrible problem with mice in the synagogue. Traps, cheese, pest control. Nothing works."

The second rabbi says, "Same thing with us. We tried it all. Still we have mice."

The third rabbi says, "We had the same problem—but not anymore!" Now the other two rabbis are interested. "How did you do it?"

It seems many religions have a hard time keeping their converts engaged, particularly in the United States. Judaism seems to have one of the best retention rates! I assume the retention rate is likely due to how difficult it is to convert in the first place—you have to be absolutely certain you want to do it. I have heard many rabbis state that the enthusiasm brought by Jews by Choice is contagious, and they are many times more observant than born Jews. However, I was asked to consider why a Jew by Choice might have difficulty after conversion.

Loss of Family

One issue that can certainly cause a rift, is between Jews by Choice and their Gentile family members. Conversion to any religion is not easy, and parents might feel they somehow failed and take conversion as a rejection of them and their faith. Your family might be perfectly accepting.

However, other people's families might not be. I have a Hasidic Jew by Choice friend whose parents are all perfectly fine with their son being an Orthodox Jew, although my friend's brother is not ok with the conversion. For me, none of my family is particularly happy. If you are particularly close to your family, this can be devastating! Some might choose to stop practicing Judaism in order to appease parents. I have not cared about those issues, so I did not worry.

Loss of Friends

Another friend called the loss of friends, the "flight of the goyim." Many Gentiles might no longer wish to associate with you, either because they do not know how to communicate with you or they might not understand why some of your behaviors have changed, such as no longer

---

"It was easy. I went to the sanctuary, gathered all the mice together, made them come up to the bima, and performed a mass bar mitzvah. And we haven't seen any of them since!"

wanting to come over for Easter dinner! I have been accused of horrible things by people who believe I am an extreme Zionist in order to score "Judaism points," when I am a supporter and have been a supporter for many years of peace between Israelis and the Palestinian people. Yes, I love Israel (Zion), but I am hardly one to wish unnecessary harm on others which is what many people believe Zionists want.

If you become shomer Shabbat, many activities on Friday evening and Saturday afternoon (days when many people hang out with their friends) might become difficult. If you decide to keep very strict kosher, this could also cause difficulties. However, this also occurs even among born Jews who are more observant than their family members.

It's a Whole New World

As a Jew by Choice, you are often expected to adopt an entirely new culture, and it can be very difficult. There will be social and religious faux pas regardless of if you were born Jewish or are a Jew by Choice. That is simply part of life. However, many born Jews, in my experience, take a particular delight in attempting to be harsher on Jews by Choice than they are on born Jews.

The Torah states one should be kind to the stranger, however this does not always occur. I am not sure if this is ignorance on their part or if there is a tendency to want to think of Jews by Choice as being second class since they needed to work to earn their Jewish status.

Language Issues

Jews have a variety of languages. Hebrew, Yiddish, and Ladino are the three main non-English languages. Depending on the synagogue, the services could be entirely in Hebrew, entirely in English, or a mixture of anything.

People might communicate with each other in English, Hebrew, Yiddish, Ladino, or whatever other language is common, depend-ing on the neighborhood and not knowing the language could cause tremendous difficulties. Even when English is spoken, like many other cultures, there are sometimes drastically different (sometimes opposite) meanings depending on which word is stressed.

No Longer Getting Rabbi's Time

When one is in the process of conversion, rabbis and teachers will spend a lot of time with their students. However, when one is out of the mikvah, many times the attention stops. However, the mikvah should not be the end of a Jew by Choice's education any more than a bar mitzvah should be the end of a Jew's education. In many ways, this is the time that the Jews by Choice, especially the ones who do not have Jewish family members, need guidance the most.

After the mikvah, the Jew by Choice is now a Jewish adult responsible for all of the mitzvot and may have more questions than they had prior to the conversion. This could cause someone to have more questions but no one willing to answer their halacha question!

Mixed Attitudes Toward Converts

Like it or not, there will be mixed attitudes toward Jews by Choice assuming people know you are a Jew by Choice. Some might state Jews by Choice are great, and others might insist on treating them like second-class Jews. If a Jew by Choice is not aware of this as a possibility, they might not know how to react if it comes up. They might doubt themselves or doubt their conversion and stop practicing because they might feel that they never were Jewish in the first place. This will be discussed further.

Identity Issues

Another problem simply can be the difficulties with other parts of identities. I know an Orthodox Jew by Choice who is gay and finding it very difficult to merge these parts together. He feels like he either has to choose to be gay or choose to be an Orthodox Jew. Sometimes it can be very difficult when one has identities that are a challenge to merge. This happens in many areas, not just relating to conversion issues.

It Can Be Hard to Be Jewish

613. There are 613 mitzvot, not including minhagim (customs) that one needs to work around. It is very hard to monitor all of those mitzvot, even though many of them are not active. Not to mention the possibility of people simply not liking Jewish people. It can become incredibly overwhelming.

Realizing Many Born Jews Are Not Observant

While realizing other Jews might not be observant might not be the first thing that one thinks of as something that could drive away Jews by Choice, it can happen. Of course, this could depend on where you are and who you are with. I was invited to an Orthodox family's home.

I felt very awkward whispering blessings over food or touching the mezuzah when no one else in the family did. I found myself questioning what it was that I was supposed to be doing at any one point. It was equally bothersome when I met someone else who was raised Orthodox but only went to synagogue four times a year when he was growing up.

What Are You Going to Do with the Conversion?

A friend of mine suggested this section for the book, and I have to admit that I was at first very confused as to what she was referring to. The question, "What are you going to do with the conversion?" with her lips pursed reminds me of individuals asking what a student is going to do with a certain major once they get out of college. However, I have never heard a person converting to another religion, such as Catholicism, to justify what they were going to do with their conversion.

Of course, conversion to Judaism is different from a conversion to other religions. Judaism is, after all, referred to as the world's smallest global family. Just like in many families, there are things that you will allow your family members to do that you might not allow strangers or even friends to do. Judaism is not much different in this regard.

Conversion gives you some rights that Gentiles might not have in Jewish circles. While, of course, conversion allows you to read from the Torah, be given an aliyah, and be honored and recognized when Jewish family members become bar or bat mitzvah, there are other things.

In communities with a high Jewish population, when one has a legal disagreement with another Jew one could, instead of going directly to a secular court, one could instead be judged by a religious court (beit din). Depending on the nature of the disagreement, the beit din could be more lax or more strict than the secular court. Also given the religious nature of the court, there might be areas where a secular court cannot rule.

Further, there are some charities, such as by providing non-interest loans, which only Jews are eligible to apply. As for not charging interest, that is because it is prohibited to charge interest to other Jews. I would hope that the reasons for a conversion would not include obtaining financial assistance.

Of course, another benefit to conversion is the ability to move to Israel. Under the Law of Return, Jews by Choice have the right to move to Israel. It is a misconception that only Orthodox are allowed to make aliyah. According to the Miller Precedent, both Reform and Conservative Jews by Choice are also allowed to make aliyah.

However, Jews by Choice who make aliyah sometimes report difficulties with getting married in Israel by Orthodox rabbis as well as being buried in Israel. Born Israelis who identify as secular often have similar difficulties, so the marriage and burial issues are not specific to Jews by Choice.

I have to admit, when I was first asked the question about what I was going to do with my conversion, my first thoughts included "continue to live a Jewish life as I did before the conversion." It was only a few minutes later that I added my second thoughts of "maybe move to Israel in a few years."

The first one did not require me to have a conversion, as I could have lived as a Jew without actually becoming one. The second reason, however, is dependent on a conversion. As of the time of this writing, I have not made aliyah, although the more I am exposed to antisemitic behavior, the more I like the idea of Israel!

Antisemitism

Jews have been persecuted throughout history, so it should come as no surprise to anyone considering conversion that there is the possibility you might become the victim of antisemitism.

You do not even need to be Jewish before you become a victim of antisemitic behavior. Some Gentiles simply do not like Jews and will target anyone who looks or acts in a way they might consider Jewish. Unfortunately, this might happen regardless of what you do or how you act. If you are perceived as being a Jew, you might get attention that you do not want to have. I have been perceived as a Jew or having Jew-like qualities since I was nine years old, which is the first time an antisemitic slur was used against me.

If you are lucky, it will only be words. If you are unlucky, it could involve more than that. I can think of several events where Jewish students were attacked on college campuses. In one case in 2012, a nineteen-year-old Michigan State University student attending a party was attacked because he was Jewish by others claiming to be members of the KKK. He had his mouth stapled shut and nothing was done to bring the perpetrators to justice. The police in fact claimed to investigate, but then stated he was lying despite all the presented evidence and witnesses. In 2015, a similar situation happened to me on the grounds of a local medical school campus where I was also attacked and insulted for being Jewish on multiple occasions. I was considered "provoking" by wearing a kippah. No one was willing to investigate claiming it was my fault. There are also attacks outside of college campuses. Many synagogues now have various forms of security, which are around at all times in order to prevent problems. In the early 21st century, there was an increase in hate crimes directed toward Jews. This cannot be driven home far enough.

Further, if you are interviewing for things such as jobs or advanced education, you may encounter people saying cruel things. I had one interviewer at a medical school tell me (in 2013) that they only had one Jew in the entire school and that was enough! Don't be surprised if such things occur. Statements like these happened time and time again when I was interviewing for medical school, and even after I was accepted, as I mentioned above, I was attacked on campus for wearing a kippah.

Discrimination from Fellow Jews

Discrimination goes further than just Gentiles against Jews. As a Jew by Choice, you may even face discrimination from fellow Jews as well.

One phenomena includes the process of conversion itself and who accepts your conversion. As has been mentioned, the Orthodox do not accept non-Orthodox conversions even if the ger did everything that was required under halacha. The only things required are education (if an adult), circumcision (if male), beit din, and mikvah. Plus, of course, the naming ceremony which as far as I can tell is not required under halacha, although it certainly helps.

However, there is something even more interesting than that. Sometimes the Orthodox do not accept each other's conversions. Orthodox Jews believe the mitzvot are binding. If one of the beit din members is found to be violating a mitzvah during a time period, all their conversions may be called into question.

The conversion batei din they sat on may become void and the ger might be required to reconvert. Additionally, if a Jew by Choice is found to be in violation of a mitzvah, this could also cause the conversion itself to be called into question due to the Jew by Choice's behavior, and there could be a judgment stating the convert lied that they were willing to keep the mitzvot. This does not mean other rabbis have to accept the ruling. However, it can lead to stress for any Jew by Choice who happens to find themselves at the wrong end of the investigation!

Even if you do not convert Orthodox, you could still find yourself at the mercy of born Jews who are happy to treat you poorly because you were not born to the appropriate mother to be Jewish by birth under halacha. Some patrilineal Jews have similar issues with discrimination.

I have heard of Jews by Choice who are not allowed to help in the preparation of food for the sole reason that they were not born Jewish! This seems to be a bigger problem in more liberal congregations where some do not understand that, after the mikvah, Jews by Choice are considered to be the same as born Jews.

As a religious nation, Israel has her own set of discriminatory practices, many of which come down to who is or is not a Jew according to the Orthodox. For many years, Jews by Choice who converted in a liberal movement were not allowed to move to Israel. In a case brought before the Israeli Supreme Court, there was a ruling that Reform and Conservative Jews by Choice were allowed to make aliyah.

The adjustment to the Law of Return is called The Miller Precedent. However, given Reform and Conservative Jews are considered "secular Jews" and, at the time of this writing, only a few Reform and Conservative rabbis are being recognized in Israel and allowed to do anything recognized by the state of Israel, this causes difficulties for Reform and Conservative Jews. Even many born-Jewish Israelis must go out of the country in order to get married because they do not meet the criteria set forth to be married in Israel. Orthodox Jews are also more likely to obtain exemption from the Israeli Defense Forces as well as get paid to study and even get free or low-cost housing.

SPECIAL TOPICS

Converting on a Budget

Converting to Judaism can be expensive, and if one does not have a lot of disposable income it can be important to take advantage of free or low-cost resources when possible. I was on food stamps and was unemployed during the last few years of my conversion process, so I learned many ways to stretch the dollar while continuing on the process of conversion.

Education

As you recall, there is going to be an extensive process of education prior to conversion. This process will include formal classes as well as outside independent learning. This is an excellent place to start because there are so many resources out there that are low cost.

Friendship with other Jews is free. Of course, finding friends can be difficult if you are not a social butterfly. If you are one of those lucky people who are able to acquire friends easily, just go to shul and in no time you will meet people.

If you are not a very social person, your rabbi might be able to set you up with a mentor or mentor family who can help supplement your education and teach you and guide you as to living Jewishly. Friends who know you are interested in converting can be a way into the community and can provide many chances for you to explore Judaism.

Many rabbis require an introduction to Judaism course that likely is not free. However, that does not mean it is impossible to take if you are converting on a budget. My teacher allowed for a payment plan which helped tremendously since I only had to put down a small deposit.

Thanks to the payment plan, when some family members asked what I wanted for the holidays, I told them I wanted the next installment of my class paid for. I was very lucky in that regard. You might even be able to take the class in exchange for bartering your skills in some way. Your rabbi even might offer to pay for the class.

Of course, you may have outside reading. Depending on your financial situation, there are many options. The first option is to borrow books from friends or the library. Depending on where you live, you might find the public library lacking in Jewish books. However, they might be able to request an interlibrary loan if there is something specific that you wish to read.

Another library option is your synagogue, which may have a library or learning center where you can check out books of interest. Further, with the rise of the internet and e-readers, you can find many public domain books for free. Amazon has dozens if not hundreds of Jewish books available for free for their Kindle reader. The best part of Kindle is that you do not need a Kindle to read the books. You can download the books to a computer to read later. Free public domain books can be found through Google books.

For those who have spare money, used books are an option. I am a fan of book trading websites where you mail books out and get books in return. I have received hundreds of books through these methods, although Jewish books can be a challenge since many of them are highly sought after. Generally when you add shipping, these books are usually cheaper to receive than purchasing through Amazon and sometimes cheaper than purchasing from a thrift store. Of course, Amazon and other online retailers are your best option for purchasing a wider variety of books.

Education can also consist of movies. Of course you can wait for movies of Jewish interest to come on the television, assuming you have a television or satellite or cable, but for those who do not there are still other options. The public library or your synagogue's library might have movies to borrow. Also, is the timing right for your city's Jewish Film Festival?

However, there are also other options as well. If you have a good internet connection, several websites offer streaming movies. Unfortunately, it can be difficult to assess their selection until you register. Luckily, many have a free trial that you can use. When I signed up for a free one-month subscription to one of the big name streaming services, I went on a movie watching rampage and watched nearly all their Jewish interest movies within the month. Then I canceled it before the trial was finished. I could not justify going beyond it since I already watched all of the movies I wanted to watch. I would not renew my membership for another ten years when, ironically, there were almost no Jewish films on it anymore.

The internet is a huge source of information, both good and bad. There are websites like Chabad, My Jewish Learning, and Aish. There are also tons of blogs, podcasts, and news sources. There is nothing you cannot find on the internet. The only difficult thing is sorting through what is a good source and what is a bad source of information.

Beit Din

The beit din should be relatively low cost unless you have to travel to get to them. Generally, a handmade item or a card will suffice if you wish to give a gift. I gave all of mine a gift card and challah.

Circumcision

If a man needs a circumcision, it would be best performed by a medical doctor. Unfortunately, unless there is a medical reason to be circumcised, insurance might consider this an elective procedure. This might make them unlikely to pay. However, there is always the possibility of negotiating doctor's fees. Talk to the individual physician to see what they say.

Mikvah

The mikvah I used served as the mikvah for all non-Orthodox conversions, and the shul asked for a donation for its use. Since I did not have money, I started looking at other options to try to save. Through my research, I found many people in my area used lakes, hot tubs, or even pools.

So as long as these options met the minimum standards to be a kosher mikvah, rabbis could allow these as options. However, when I made the suggestion of using a lake not far from me or trying to find a lake closer to the synagogue to reduce their travel time, I was pleasantly surprised to hear my rabbi tell me he would be happy to cover the cost!

Shul Memberships

One thing that might be asked of you is to join a synagogue. However, this might not be required. It depends on the rabbi and the synagogue's policies. Services can be attended without ever paying a membership fee. Assuming membership is required, there might be special member rates.

This could include student rates or young adult memberships that are just a fraction of the cost of a full membership. They might even offer a free membership if you have not been previously associated with a synagogue, although while Jews by Choice tend to qualify for this, the synagogues are primarily reaching out for unaffiliated born Jews who drifted away from Judaism. Additionally, if you really cannot afford a full-cost membership fee, see if your synagogue will work with you and give you a discounted fee.

One benefit to a shul membership for the prospective Jew by Choice relates to High Holy Day tickets. Since they can be expensive and difficult to acquire, a membership often gets you access to the services. However, it is possible to obtain free tickets if needed. Some tzedakah tickets are set aside for students and individuals who might not be able to afford tickets.

Additionally, some services will give you free tickets if you volunteer to help usher. My first High Holy Day services were all given to me for free: one free service for the Erev Rosh Hashanah, two Rosh Hashanah tzedakah tickets (different synagogues on different days), free ticket for Kol Nidre (I ushered although my prior tzedakah ticket for that synagogue would have covered it), and another tzedakah ticket for Yom Kippur day for a different synagogue.

Getting Judaica

There is no rule stating that you must purchase large amounts of Judaica. It is amazing how little you actually need. Things can be reappropriated, such as candlesticks which can be used for Shabbat. A paper plate can be decorated and used as a temporary seder plate for Passover.

If you are expected to separate milk and meat dishes, many of your old ones might be able to be immersed in a mikvah instead of needing to purchase a new set.

Furthermore, there is the possibility of getting things as gifts, paying for things on barter, or trying to find appropriate things in a thrift store. I would be hesitant to purchase too much used Judaica through thrift stores due to Jewish superstitions. Most things, however, you will not need to purchase right away. Anything you do need to purchase, such as mezuzah scrolls and such, can be comparison shopped online.

Kosher Eating

You might choose to keep kosher starting at your conversion, before your conversion, or you might choose to not keep kosher at all depending on your converting movement. People who want to keep kosher learn very quickly that it can be expensive.

For part of the time I was in conversion, I was living on $50 for groceries per month, which was the most I could afford to spend and part of that included food for service animals. I later qualified for food stamps, which increased the amount I could spend and assured I did not starve. Some of this advice is not specific to eating kosher foods.

1) Look outside the kosher section.

Most grocery stores have an ethnic food section, and frequently there is a section within that section called "kosher." This area frequently contains items like matzah ball soup, hummus, gefilte fish, and other stereotypically Jewish foods. This section also often contains Shabbat candles.

Despite the fact a food is under the kosher section, the food might not be kosher, so check for the hechsher if this is important to you. The food might not be kosher because the store employees misplaced the food or made assumptions about where it needed to go. I usually double check brands I have never seen before. Israeli products are almost always kosher even if you don't see a recognizable hechsher.

If you are shopping by hechsher, a large amount of brand name foods throughout the store are certified as kosher. There are even many store brands which carry a hechsher. Imagine my surprise when I was looking at generic brands in order to save money and found many of them had a hechsher!

2) Check clearance and manufacturer's specials.

Not every store has this, but some have a specific location where there are reduced prices. Matzah ball soup, which usually costs a fortune, I purchased for 50% off because my store was clearing out inventory. My favorite grocery store in the Toco Hills section of Atlanta has at least two clearance sections for shelf-stable products, one is all kosher and the other is partially kosher. You can acquire not only food, but also Shabbat candles.

3) Sign up for loyalty programs, as they can give you discounts.

With shopping smart and a loyalty card, I purchased over $60 worth of food for just over $20 dollars. I saved $40.05 according to my receipt, and only $1.50 were in coupons. The rest was the loyalty card and being able to time my shopping to get the best deals. Everything purchased was kosher. Saving $20 or more is not unusual.

4) Consider using coupons.

You do not have to be an extreme couponer, but every little bit helps.

5) Buy in bulk.

Since I bake a lot of challah, I buy a large container of five dozen eggs at a time because it is cheaper per egg. Cream cheese, I buy 10 for $10 and put it in the freezer. I bought four very large containers of sour cream for $5 a few weeks ago and they are now in my freezer (yes it destroys the texture so that might not work for you, but works when I cook with it). I would normally get one small sour cream for about $3. I will buy a gallon of milk and divide it into smaller containers and freeze most of it.

6) Consider purchasing generics or store brands that have a hechsher.

Do not blindly assume a generic is going to be cheaper, because sometimes it isn't. Do not blindly assume generics are not kosher, because they might be. Check the price per unit. Check for a hechsher. Of course if the generics are really bad (some are), then do not waste the money.

7) Try to bake from scratch.

There is no bakery in my area that sells challah regularly. I cannot even request it. Even if I could purchase it, the local bakeries are not supervised by the local Kashrut association, so learning how to bake became important. So instead I make my own bread by hand. Instead of paying $4 per loaf for challah, which is the current rate, I am probably doing it for well under $1 per loaf.

I only purchase bread if I can get it for less than 50 cents if it is white bread or $1 if it is any form of specialty bread. I admit I use mixes for cakes and do not bake them completely from scratch, but the mixes usually cost me only about $1.50 or less. They have hechshers.

7) Fruits and veggies... eat lots of fresh fruits and veggies.

Fruits and vegetables do not require a hechsher and are considered parve, neither milk nor meat. Not only are they kosher, but they are good for you too! Anything excess can be canned and stored for later assuming you have that equipment.

8) Be creative with leftovers.

Be creative so you do not let food go to waste. I had a lunch that consisted of tea, some eggplant parmesan from Shabbat, excess cauliflower from two nights prior, and some weird pumpkin thing for dessert that I had made the previous week.

9) Reduce meat intake.

Kosher meat tends to be very expensive. When you are far from a kosher butcher, the travel time and gas costs can further eat up your time and money. I solved this problem, as many others do, by reducing meat intake. I primarily eat meat only on Shabbat.

This does not mean I don't eat fish, which is parve, just kosher meat alone. When I am in the area of a kosher butcher, I pop my head in and check for any manager's specials. If there are some, I purchase what I can and freeze it. Then I defrost what I need for the next Shabbat.

10) Decide on which hechsher (or hechshers) you accept.

There are over 600 hechshers in the United States, although only a few dominate the food market. The most well known is Orthodox Union. I know an Orthodox family who will only accept this hechsher. I have a much wider range of hechshers and this allows me to have access to a wider variety of food.

One of the hechshers I accept, Triangle K, has periodically been in the news for certifying meat as kosher that some groups do not consider kosher. This is because some groups of Jews believe only glatt kosher meats should be certified as kosher. I am less worried about whether or not something is glatt or not. Besides, the only kosher meat that is available in a forty-mile radius from my house, Hebrew National Hotdogs, is currently certified by Triangle K. Triangle K is considered an acceptable hechsher in Israel for meat products. If it is good enough for Israel, it is good enough for me.

Another thing to consider is this. Will you accept food that is kosher by ingredients but simply have not been identified as kosher?

Acquiring a hechsher can be expensive, so if I do not see a hechsher, but it is something that I need to have, I read the ingredients list very carefully in order to see if I can find if there is a reason why the item is not kosher. I then make a judgment call to purchase or not based on the information I learned.

Being LGBT and a JBC

I've always hated it when people ask me why it took me so long to convert to Judaism. In order to answer that question honestly, I have to come out as being transgender. Yes, as you will see in my sample conversion essay and may or may not have noticed, I am not only transgender but gay as well. This has been a tremendous stepping stone in my own conversion process mostly just dealing with discrimination. If you are LGBT, this might cause difficulties if you also feel the need to convert.

Like in any other area of life, some people are more open to LGBT individuals than others. Judaism is no exception. First, let me state that it is very hard to convert Orthodox if you are gay. That is not to say that some rabbis will not do it, as I have heard through the grapevine of LGBT-friendly Orthodox rabbis who help facilitate conversions.

One of these rabbis I have spoken to, so I know he exists. However, if you are LGBT you might want to safely assume that the Orthodox movement will be less friendly to you. It can also be difficult to remain Orthodox if you are gay and were born Jewish. Some communities use therapy or conversion therapy to try to talk people out of being gay. Many of the patients end up leaving Orthodoxy or committing suicide. However, there are a few groups such as Eshel that focus solely on supporting LGBT Orthodox Jews.

While the Conservative movement varies and has certainly been progressing, I have experienced discrimination specifically due to not being gender conforming. As a female-to-male transsexual, I was very much a tomboy before I transitioned, and this was held against me when I wanted to convert Conservative.

Despite the fact I was dating men, the rabbi assumed I was a lesbian, and he stated he could not convert a gay person. This caused me so much grief that I tried running away from Judaism for years. Even in 2012, my conversion was not accepted by the Conservative movement.

The rest of the movements, Reform, Reconstructionist, Renewal, and Humanistic, are more likely to be accepting of the LGBT community. Reconstructionists are well known for being the most LGBT-friendly movement, however despite the fact there are straight people that attend Reconstructionist services, many people will just assume you are gay if you are Reconstructionist. There are a lot of Reform synagogues (and a few Conservative) that include LGBT people and even boast about their LGBT inclusivity.

However, that does not mean that the synagogues are all aware of and took LGBT Issues 101, particularly if one of their congregants is transgender. I have heard several transgender people who are Jews by Choice complain that they were asked what their birth name was even though it was not their legal name.

Rabbis are human, and many of them are just as oblivious as many other straight people. If rabbis press you for information that you feel is not relevant, then consider speaking to a different rabbi. The only thing I feel that a rabbi has the right to know is whether you do or do not have a penis, and that is only due to the requirement of circumcision.

I was very lucky, I think, despite the fact I may have been the first transgender person my sponsoring rabbi converted, the only question that was weird was the circumcision question, which I think honestly is going to be weird for almost anyone. He kept forgetting the answer to if I was or was not circumcised.

One issue that transgender people might have relates to what gender to convert as. It is very tempting to state without thinking that it is obvious one wants to convert as one's appropriate gender and not one's sex assigned at birth. However, this is one of the reasons it is important to pick a sponsoring movement.

As of 2016, the Orthodox and Conservative movements state the gender of an individual is decided according to the external genitalia. If you have not had genital surgery, this could cause a problem. The position of the Reform and Reconstructionist movements state the gender is determined according to what is in one's head. Further, if you convert as your sex assigned at birth, a new conversion might need to occur or a new conversion certificate drawn up in the event your sex is changed and you wish to make aliyah.

I read a situation where an Orthodox Jew by Choice converted as female, had surgery and had all gender markers changed, and was not allowed to make aliyah until his original beit din reissued a corrected conversion certificate stating he was a male. I personally have one issue. I converted Reform as a male, but I want more children.

This begs the question as to who the mother of my child would be given that I would likely be considered their father instead of their mother, and I do not personally recognize patrilineal descent! Whether my child would be recognized as a matrilineal Jew still bothers me, and I do not know what I would do in the event I decide to have another child. The Reform movement would not reconvert the child, as the child is already considered Jewish. The status of future children might be something that might be a concern for you.

However, for those who think they are truly alone in being gender nonconforming, it might be interesting to note that in the Talmud, there are six different halachic categories, four of them not completely male or female.[6]

Being a Rural Jew Without Community

When I converted, I was the county Jew. At least, I didn't meet a single Jew who lived within an hour during the nearly ten years I lived there. Given my dog was named Corky (a typical Jewish name) before I rescued him, one would assume there was at least one other Jewish family somewhere in the area.

However, if there was another family, they were in hiding. To give some idea of how few Jews there were out there (or potentially how lazy the local Kroger was), I remember purchasing some matzah ball soup and a box of matzah. A month went by and not only were the products not replaced, no other items had been taken from the very small kosher shelf in the ethnic section. Finally, six weeks after my purchase, it was restocked.

---

[6]   These categories are Androgynos, Tumtum, Ay'lonit, and Saris.

For someone like me who came from the Miami/Fort Lauderdale area, the culture shock when I first moved to Georgia to attend Oxford College was amazing. When I tried to purchase a menorah and some gelt for Hanukkah, the sales associates neither at Target nor at the two Walmarts I visited understood what I was asking for. When I explained what the items were, things used for Jewish holidays, they directed me toward the "juice" section.

I spent over a decade as a Jew without community, something unfathomable to most Jews, all while still keeping biblical kosher as best I could and living in an environment where everything seemed designed to destroy everyone who wasn't a Christian. I remember performing Jewish rituals I had learned as a child and forgetting why I was doing them. The memories I had of them were so far away it might as well have just been a dream.

It took three years before I met my first Jew in Georgia, then another six years before I met my second, then another two years before I met my third. A friend of mine (a potential Jew by Choice) did not meet his first Jew in person until he was fifty-three years old. Not knowing any Jewish people for fifty-three years was about as unfathomable to me as my living without a Jewish community is unfathomable to most Jews, since Jewish life is focused on family and community.

The most important thing I have found in order to keep some semblance of identity is to find a community online if you cannot find a local community. While there might not be any Jews in your local area, there is no reason to think you cannot contact other Jews online. Blogging sites, Facebook, Twitter, etc are all great places to connect with other Jewish people.

My friend who only met his first real life Jew at the age of fifty-three at least communicated with others via Twitter. He also claims he made a lot of new Jewish friends from eBay when he was purchasing items from Israel. The only problem is that like on the internet, people might not always be what they claim, and it is easy for people to troll others.

Blogging sites often have many Jewish communities where all you have to do is search for people and communities who have interests related to what you are searching for. For example, if you are searching for a community for Jews by Choice, you might want to search for terms such as Judaism, Jewish By Choice, Jews By Choice, or converting to Judaism. A listing of communities to join should be available. Many other social media sites, even those that are not specifically blogs have groups. There might even be in person meetups.

There are also wonderful informative blog sites out there. When I was converting, I heavily used "You're Not Crazy" (http://crazyjewish-convert.blogspot.com which I was just notified that Skylar is expecting to move her site to http://www.buildingajewishlife.com), which although it is heavily based on converting (or becoming) Orthodox, I owe a lot to Skylar Curtis, the blogger who runs the site.

She helped answer some of the questions I had (although from an Orthodox point of view) when no one else would answer any questions at all! Unfortunately, at the time of this writing, she has not been posting as regularly as she once was, however I hope she is able to return soon and luckily she is leaving her archives up. If you have the time or the interest, I would recommend reading through her blog site, because I consider it valuable even if you are not converting Orthodox. There is also Jewlicious, which is one of the larger Jewish blog sites, although not conversion specific.

There are also other great Jewish specific online resources depending on what you need. Are you interested in having access to knowing what is going on in the Jewish world? There are websites such as "The Jewish Daily Forward," which provide ample opportunity to learn more about what is going on in the Jewish world from a news perspective. If you are on Facebook or other social networking sites, there are multiple Jewish and Israeli fan pages which post Jewish news.

For those of you who want to watch services, but attending Friday night services is difficult, there are synagogues, primarily Reform, which stream services. You can search for further streaming services for "streaming Shabbat services."

For example, Temple Sinai in Atlanta Georgia is a "Reform leaning toward Traditional" synagogue based in Sandy Springs Georgia. They stream Friday and Saturday services. In the interest of full disclosure, my sponsoring rabbi was the senior rabbi of this synagogue, and one of my other beit din members came from this synagogue. I also used OurJewishCommunity, which was a Humanistic website streaming Friday nights.

While I personally enjoy learning from and listening to Humanistic rabbis, I realize that many movements do not respect Humanistic Judaism because Humanistic has less of a focus on religion and G-d. I am including it because I believe everyone should be able to make their own decisions, and I have enjoyed sitting in on their services in the past. Temple Beth-El is a Conservative synagogue based out of Springfield, Massachusetts, and I streamed their Saturday morning Shabbat services on days I felt like watching a Conservative service.

If you do not wish to stream, there are other options as well. iTunes has many synagogue podcasts listed as well as other educational Jewish material. All you have to do is type Jewish or Judaism in the search box.

One of the great challenges for a Jew by Choice if you are living in a rural community is not necessarily the lack of access to a community in general, but also the lack of access to a rabbi.

It is one thing to stream services and communicate with other Jews online, but it is another thing to try to convert when you live far enough away that either you cannot find a sponsoring rabbi at all or your sponsoring rabbi has concerns about you being able to participate in Jewish life.

Unfortunately, there will always be rabbis who will not convert someone who does not live in the heart of a Jewish community. I know one Jew by Choice who was required to move to New York before she was allowed to convert.

I was lucky. While I was originally told that my sponsoring rabbi was unlikely to entertain the thought of converting someone who lived so far away, when I spoke to him and played a bit of Jewish Geography with him (including how I was referred to him by a friend of his from seminary), he was willing. While we met for the first time in the synagogue, the rest of our meetings were via Skype. We did not see each other again in person until the conversion itself.

When I was converting, the issue of distance came up several times during my beit din meeting. You have to find some way to convince the beit din that not only are you going to be a good Jew, but that you will find a way to be involved in the local Jewish community and be active in the life of the synagogue you eventually become a member of. If that means you have to drive in every few weeks for a Jewish event or a service or a Shabbat dinner, then you need to tell them this.

Being Disabled and a JBC

Let's face it, if you have a disability—whether it is obvious or invisible—it plays a part in your life. Certainly, it may play a part in your conversion as well. Luckily, there are also prayer books that are in Braille for the blind. A few synagogues also offer interpreters for the deaf.

There are certain things that you might need to address with your rabbi that might be specific to your individual disability. Since Judaism does not place an obstacle before the blind (literally it is in the Torah), the rabbis will generally find a way to help you. For example, someone who needs a walker or a wheelchair may have difficulties getting to services and may have problems getting into the mikvah for conversion.

Luckily, with the Americans with Disabilities Act, many synagogues are now wheelchair accessible. Some synagogues allow a streaming service, which may be a good fit. I have also heard of different ways the mikvah can be altered so that someone may transfer into a seat and get lowered into the water and have a companion help with the immersions.

I myself have a small host of difficulties including epilepsy, ADHD, an auditory processing disorder, and being on the autistic spectrum. The fact that one seizure can make me unable to drive for six months can cause a tremendous problem for a culture so bound by the nature of community.

The autism spectrum disorder caused there to be questions raised about my ability to convert. This actually was the reason one rabbi (rabbi number 4) dropped me as a student, despite Ashkenazi Jews having one of the highest rates of autism spectrum disorders in the world.

Luckily, I found a place willing to give me some time to myself and reach out when ready. I was able to make a few friends in one of the largest synagogues in the United States. The only thing that did not get worked with very well was my auditory processing problem and general tone-deafness, which makes my ability to recite prayers in tune with the congregation a bit of a challenge.

Additionally, the strobes and flashes when people are taking photos, which is not only a Shabbat violation but also distracting in general, have caused me to have auras. The rabbis are aware of this, but the congregants and other staff however do not seem to care, proving selfishness occurs in Judaism as well. The High Holy Days remain miserable for me.

Being of a Different Race and Being a JBC

As someone who is mixed race (part Surinamese Creole for those keeping score), but is more European than anything else, I am lucky that this is an issue that I personally don't have to worry about nearly as much as others. If I say I'm Jewish, no one is going to question it simply due to the color of my skin. Although it helps that I look like I could be a born-Jew, as I have a Middle Eastern look to me.

In the United States, most Jews are white... mostly either from Germany or Eastern Europe. There are so few Jews of Color here, I have heard of nightmarish things being said to Jews of Color such as being denied the right for an aliyah or such because no one believed they were Jewish. I heard of one African American Jew (whose maternal grandmother was Jewish) who was continuously denied his right for an aliyah because no one at the synagogue in which he was a member believed he was Jewish even though he spoke fluent Hebrew and was a yeshiva graduate!

In Israel, there is a much wider range of racial diversity among Jews as there are many Jews from Ethiopia, India, China, South Africa, etc. Israel shows Jews come in all shapes, sizes, and colors. In my case, I am descended from someone whose father was a Sephardic Jew and mother was a black Jew, and that relative married an Ashkenazi Jew, which produced my great grandfather on my maternal grandmother's side. My Surinamese Creole side was Jewish.

The only advice I can truly provide is to feel out the synagogue. If they make you feel uncomfortable, don't stay. If the rabbi makes you feel uncomfortable, don't stay. Find out how many other Jews of Color they have in their synagogue. The most important thing is that you feel comfortable.

Converting a Child

In many ways converting a child is much simpler than converting an adult. Many will be converted as infants or as young children. Any education they should have in order to function as a Jew, they are simply too young to learn and will be taught at the same time that born-Jewish children are taught. The process therefore simply requires a circumcision (if male), a mikvah, and the naming ceremony.

There are several things that need to be considered when converting a child. Are both of the parents agreeable to the conversion? If one is and one isn't, an agreement must be made one way or the other, perhaps also with consultation from a rabbi. If the parents are divorced, this could make it very difficult, as the parents, who may be of different religions, compete for the child's love and attention and could end up confusing the child.

Another thing that must be considered is that the child ethically will have to know they were converted. Before the age of thirteen for a boy and twelve for a girl, the child needs to be told he or she was converted so he or she may accept or reject the conversion. If the child accepts the conversion or remains silent, the child remains Jewish. If not, the child reverts back to being a Gentile. In this way, it is like a temporary conversion to wait for the child to really understand what was given to them. My mother was converted to Catholicism as a child, but they do not have the ability to throw off their conversion.

I would suggest if you convert a child, and really this should go for born-Jewish children as well, don't do anything to make your child hate the religion. You want children who are proud to be Jewish.

Converting When Your Spouse Is Not Jewish

I know at least three people, myself included, who converted when married to a non-Jewish spouse. Let me state that I feel this is not an ideal situation but one that sometimes cannot be helped. Many rabbis also simply will not entertain the thought of converting one spouse and not the other. After all this creates an interfaith family, which should be avoided to the best of one's ability.

If the spouse is Jewish, even another Jew by Choice, the home would be united in a faith. If the spouse is not only not Jewish but not supportive, this can cause difficulties within the home.

You might have to explain to your spouse why little boxes have started appearing by your doorposts. Or you may have to deal with different reactions when it comes to splitting dishes. Compromises may need to be made, and that can impact the new Jew from fully immersing in their new faith and could provide a problem when children are introduced. This may cause an identity conflict as to what parent is the correct one, as one cannot believe in Jesus or celebrate Christian holidays and be a good Jew.

Converting to another religion could be incredibly stressful especially when one is converting to a different culture as well. If the spouse were Jewish by birth, their family may be able to help with mentoring support or such as the event of a new baby being born, can help make arrangements. Assume that if you are converting without having Jewish family, you are going to have more stress than if you had such a support structure.

APPENDIX A

JEWISH HOLIDAYS

Shabbat

Everyone who has experienced Shabbat knows it is special. Shabbat takes precedence over every other holiday except Yom Kippur. This is the one day where we may not do any work whatsoever.

In fact, there are thirty-nine different categories of work expressly forbidden to be performed on Shabbat: plowing earth, sowing, reaping, binding sheaves, threshing, winnowing, selecting, grinding, sifting, kneading, baking, shearing wool, washing wool, beating wool, dyeing wool, spinning, weaving, making two loops, weaving two threads, separating two threads, tying, untying, sewing stitches, tearing, trapping, slaughtering, flaying, tanning, scraping hide, marking hides, cutting hide to shape, writing two or more letters, erasing two or more letters, building, demolishing, extinguishing a fire, kindling a fire, putting the finishing touch on an object, and transporting an object between the private domain and the public domain or for a certain distance within the public domain.

In ancient times when Shabbat was first introduced, the average worker worked seven days a week, so this is something very different from before. While many nowadays consider a weekend two days, having simply one day off was revolutionary at the time.

Although traditional Jews pray three times a day and Shabbat is a time when many liberal Jews go to synagogue, there are additional things that occur during Shabbat. It is traditional to light at least two candles between one and a half hours to eighteen minutes before sunset.

You light the candles, wave your arms around the candles a certain amount of times (three is most common), cover your eyes, and do the blessing over the candles. From that point on, Shabbat has begun. While it is more common for a woman to perform this mitzvah of lighting candles, any adult Jew may perform it. In fact, this is one of my favorite mitzvot!

Different people have different ways of observing Shabbat. I tend to keep more shomer Shabbat than most. This is not to say I am perfect, as I do err, however I try to avoid driving on Shabbat, I do not conduct business transactions on Shabbat unless it cannot wait until Sunday, my lights either remain on or off for all of Shabbat (I even have Shabbat light switch covers), I normally tape my refrigerator light down so it does not turn on if I need to access the refrigerator, I avoid cooking on Shabbat if I can help it, and the computer tends to stay off during Shabbat.

The only thing that remains on is my phone in case G-d forbid someone needs to get a hold of me, although most people know I am not up for small talk during Shabbat. My phone would also remain on to its weather radio function and email notification function. I will answer right away if it is an emergency, if not I will wait until after Havdalah to respond. It is traditional to eat three festival meals a day during Shabbat along with meat. Given the expense of kosher meat, this is one of the few days where I can eat kosher meat. During each meal, Kiddush is to be recited and two loaves of challah are to be present. Each challah loaf with its six braids, together make twelve braids, one to represent each of the twelve tribes of Israel. The traditional greetings before Shabbat begins or during Shabbat are either Shabbat Shalom (Hebrew) or Gut Shabbos (Yiddish).

Days of Awe / Days of Repentance

It is said that Yom Kippur is the day that atones for sins between man and G-d, but not between individuals. The Days of Repentance is when Jews seek reconciliation with people they have wronged and to seek forgiveness. Traditionally, a Jew asks for forgiveness three times, if the wronged person refuses to forgive it is no longer the Jew's burden. This is also a time for reflection upon how you can be a better person for the next year.

Some Hasidic Jews also perform the custom of kapparot, though it is a rare practice, during the Days of Awe (commonly Tishrei 9). This practice involves circling a live chicken around one's head and considering it as atonement for sins. The chicken is then killed and given to the poor. This is a controversial practice due to the occasional mistreatment of the animals.

Rosh Hashanah

Rosh Hashanah is a two day festival (in the Diaspora at least, as it is one day in Israel) celebrating the Jewish New Year. The reason for it being two days is because of the Jewish calendar. During the Diaspora, Jews were scattered throughout the land, and it was difficult to know when official new moons occurred. Sometimes it took a while for the message to be relayed. Even though we now know for sure when the new moon is, some continue the tradition. Officially, both days are work restricted holidays like Shabbat.

Judaism has many New Year celebrations, and this one is the Jewish New Year for the counting of years while the others are new years for counting of trees, reigns, and cattle. Rosh Hashanah is also the Day of Judgment and the first of the Days of Awe.

On the Day of Judgment, it is said that HaShem inscribes the fate of everyone into either the Book of Life or the Book of Death for the upcoming year. During the days of Awe, Jews reflect upon themselves and try to persuade HaShem to ensure they are written in the Book of Life. The verdict is not final until Yom Kippur when the book is sealed.

During Rosh Hashanah, many Jews who would not normally attend services will be in synagogue for this as well as Yom Kippur. Rosh Hashanah tickets are frequently expensive due to demand for seating. Most of the community will be using a special prayer book called a machzor unless their siddur includes the High Holy Day service.

The central mitzvah of the holiday is hearing the shofar blast. The shofar is traditionally a very large hollowed out ram's horn. In a service there are several times when the shofar is blown, these are Teki'ah (long sound) based on Numbers 10:3; Shevarim (three broken sounds) based on Numbers 10:5; Teru'ah (nine short sounds) based on Numbers 10:9; Teki'ah Gedolah (very long sound) based on Exodus 19:16-19; Shevarim Teru'ah (three broken sounds followed by nine short sounds).

Many Jews also perform the practice of Tashlikh ("casting off"), which involves taking bread down to a living and flowing body of water in order to symbolically cast off one's sins for the new year. I remember the first year I did Tashlikh, I surprised one of my rabbis when I volunteered to go down with him on the second day of Rosh Hashanah and he asked if I knew of Tashlikh and I said "Yes, I did a little bit yesterday!"

It is also traditional to eat a festive meal, particularly a meal with round challah somewhat sweeter than normal and the dinner should include apples and honey. The apples are dipped in honey in order to symbolize a sweet new year.

The traditional greetings on Rosh Hashanah include L'shanah Tovah Tikatev V'taihatem L'Alter L'Chaim Tovim Ul'Shalom means (May you (immediately) be inscribed and sealed for a Good Year (and for a Good and Peaceful Life), Ketiva V'Chatima Tovah (May You Be Written and Sealed for a Good Year), and Tizku L'Shanim Rabot ("May You Merit Many Years"). Most commonly you will simply hear Shana Tovah (A Good Year) or Shanah Tovah Umetukah (A Good and Sweet Year).

Tzom Gedaliah

This is a minor fast day following the second day of Rosh Hashanah. During this time, it is customary to fast from dawn until three stars appear in the sky. Since it is a minor fast day, the rules on who is exempt from fasting are more lenient than on major fast days. The ill (even if the condition is not life-threatening) and pregnant or nursing women do not need to fast. This holiday is to lament the assassination of the governor Gedaliah who was killed shortly after the First Temple was destroyed.

Yom Kippur

One of the most well-known holidays on the Jewish calendar is Yom Kippur, which marks the end of the Days of Awe. Jews who normally do not attend services will generally attend services on Yom Kippur as well as on Rosh Hashanah mentioned above. Jews who only attend synagogue twice a year on these two days are frequently referred to as High Holy Day (or High Holiday) Jews.

Yom Kippur is also known as the Day of Atonement when you are atoning for your sins between yourself and G-d. After the rest of the Days of Awe, it can get wary and many people are just looking forward to it ending. This is the most difficult of all of the holidays for many. Yom Kippur is the only holiday that "outranks" Shabbat.

While both days are days where we abstain from work, this is really where the similarities end other than the fact we go to synagogue on both days. While we would normally on Shabbat eat three festive meals, on Yom Kippur, anyone old enough and healthy to fast must undergo a complete 25 hour fast during which no food or water may enter your mouth. In addition, one should not bathe, wear cosmetics or deodorants, or wear leather shoes. The traditional color of Yom Kippur is white, and many married Ashkenazi men may also wear a white robe called a kittel over their clothing.

There are exceptions to the fasting rules. Children under a certain age (around the age of nine) may not fast even partially, nor may women who are in the process of childbirth or within three days of giving birth. Slightly older children who are really preparing for the time when they will be asked to fulfill the mitzvah and women who are between three and seven days after childbirth are permitted to fast, but can break the fast if necessary.

Individuals who have medical problems, such as diabetes, should either avoid fasting altogether or enter a modified fast depending on the opinion of your rabbi and your physician. While I am not a diabetic, I am epileptic and take medication requiring water, and the condition can become aggravated by missed meals. I have done modified fasts. One consisted of half a mouthful of food every eleven minutes as was suggested by a rabbi one year and others that were fruit juice only.

Once while attempting to perform the modified fast, I was shaking so badly I refused to stop eating because I was convinced it was a medical problem. When other congregants found out I had been eating, one told me I should be ashamed of myself. When I reported this to the rabbi, he reminded me that since I take medically necessary drugs I was forbidden from fasting and to pay no mind to the congregant.

Sukkot

Five days after Yom Kippur, the holiday of Sukkot starts. We are reminded of the forty year period the Israelites wandered the desert after they were brought out of Egypt. Sukkot lasts seven days in Israel and eight in the Diaspora (the holiday of Shemini Atzeret is often considered the eighth day of Sukkot as it overlaps in Diaspora). The first two days are festival days. Sukkot is also one of the pilgrimage festivals when Jews were expected to go to Jerusalem.

This holiday is celebrated by eating in a sukkah, a temporary dwelling (somewhat resembling a walled pavilion) usually built right after Yom Kippur. It is here where we are commanded to eat and spend as much time as we can, even sleep there if possible, for the holiday.

It is also customary to decorate the sukkah to make it as lovely as possible and the decorations often involve the Seven Species: wheat, barley, grapes, figs, pomegranates, olives, and dates (which is not to be confused with the Four Species mentioned below). Further, there is a special ritual with a fruit called an etrog and a lulav. The lulav, named for the Hebrew word for palm, is made up of a palm branch, two willow branches and three myrtle branches. Together, the etrog, the palm, the willow, and the myrtle make up the Four Species. The etrog and the lulav will need to be purchased every year and should be as flawless as possible.

Shemini Atzeret and Simchat Torah

As mentioned above, in Judaism there are additional holidays that occur right after (or overlapping with) Sukkot, but are often grouped together with it. Those holidays are Shemini Atzeret and Simchat Torah.

The confusion when things fall in relation to Sukkot depends on whether one is in Israel or Diaspora as well as which movement one belongs to. Shemini Atzeret coincides with the last day of Sukkot in the Diaspora, but the day after Sukkot in Israel and in some locations it is often celebrated as a two day with Simchat Torah. Simchat Torah is celebrated on the same day as Shemini Atzeret in Israel and by some Reform and Reconstructionist Jews in the Diaspora. Simchat Torah is celebrated after Shemini Atzeret in the Diaspora by Conservative and Orthodox Jews.

On Shemini Atzeret, it is said that the Creator wished us to stay another day with Him, instead of the seven days as was originally requested. This is also the day when the world was to be judged for how much rain was going to fall in the forthcoming year. For Israel, a land in a desert, water is of particular importance, so there is always a prayer for rain for the upcoming year.

Simchat Torah, or Rejoicing of the Torah, is a very joyous celebration commemorating the celebrating the completion and new beginning of the year's Torah Reading cycle finishing the last parashah of Deuteronomy and the starting the first parashah of Genesis. It is very common to have everyone eligible for an aliyah to come and perform the blessing over the scrolls. Another common custom is to take the scrolls out of the Ark and carry them around the congregation as well as singing and dancing with the scrolls.

Hanukkah

Hanukkah, also spelled Chanukah and a variety of other spellings, is one of the most well-known holidays primarily due to its proximity to Christmas. It's an eight day festival where a special nine-branched menorah (Chanukkiyah) is used to hold an ever increasing number of candles, and the lit candles are traditionally placed near a window so the holiday might be publicized. Hanukkah is also commonly associated with food such as jelly doughnuts and latkes (potato pancakes).

Every Jewish child, and I am sure a fair amount of Gentile children, know at least part of the story of Hanukkah. Thousands of years ago, Jews were horribly oppressed under Greek rule. The Greeks even came into the Temple and sacrificed a pig on the altar.

When the Jews were able to regain control of the Temple, they started to clean, purify, and rededicate the Temple. Unfortunately, they only had enough oil to last one day. By some miracle, the day's worth of oil lasted eight days, which was enough time to create more oil. So the candles are lit to publicize the miracle of the oil lasting as long as it did. Right?

Well, that is part of the story and the story we tell the kids. The Jews were horribly oppressed under Greek rule and were not allowed to practice Judaism—that is true. Greeks likely did sacrifice pigs, as that was a relatively common practice and may have very well done at the Temple. However, when the Jewish people overcame their enemies and were allowed to practice their religion again, they started off by celebrating the most recent holiday missed, which was Sukkot, so Hanukkah was most likely a delayed Sukkot festival. I don't know about you, but I like the story of the oil better.

During Hanukkah, the most common tradition is to light candles. The first day, there is one helper candle (it is called a shamash candle, and it is raised higher than the rest) and one normal candle, the second day has a helper candle and two normal candles, and it continues until the helper candle and the eight normal candles are all lit.

When the candles are placed in the menorah, they are placed from right to left, but they are lit from left to right using the helper candle. On days when Hanukkah falls on Shabbat, the Hanukkah candles should be lit first in order to prevent kindling a flame after Shabbat has started.

A common game, primarily played on Hanukkah by Ashkenazi Jews, is dreidel, which requires a four-sided top called a dreidel that has Hebrew characters on each side. Each player has a pot of items to bet with (often chocolate coins called gelt). If a gimmel is spun (ג), the spinner gets the full pot.

If a hei is spun (ה), the spinner gets half the pot. If a nun is spun (נ), nothing happens, and if a shin is spun (ש), you put one in. Some dreidels will also have the names of the letters written on them for those who do not recognize Hebrew characters. Please note that the dreidels made in Israel tend to have a pei (פ) instead of a shin (ש).

Asara B'Tevet

This is a minor fast day on the tenth day of Tevet. During this time, it is customary to fast from dawn until three stars appear in the sky. Since it is a minor fast day like Tzom Gedaliah, the rules on who is exempt from fasting are more lenient than on major fast days. For example, the ill (even if the condition is not life-threatening) and pregnant or nursing women do not need to fast. This holiday marks the siege of Jerusalem by Nebuchadnezzar II of Babylonia. In Israel, it is often also often used as a general Kaddish day for Holocaust victims.

Tu B'Shevat

Most commonly thought of as Jewish Arbor Day, this is another one of several Jewish "New Years." Similar to how all thoroughbred horses have the same birth date of January 1st, all trees in Judaism, regardless of when they were planted, have the same birth date of Tu B'Shevat.

This practice was instituted in order to calculate tithing. A three year old tree's fruits are not allowed to be eaten and a four year old tree's fruits are considered to be for G-d and were brought as a tithe to Jerusalem. After four years, there were no restrictions as to who can use the fruit.

In keeping with the spirit of the holiday, many children will either help plant trees or will help raise money for the planting of trees in Israel. The planting of trees is so important that some traditional Jews believe if the Messiah arrives as you are going to plant a tree, you should plant the tree first and then greet the Messiah.

Another custom is a special Tu B'Shevat seder involving four glasses of wine or grape juice (each glass with a different proportion of red and white) and eating certain prescribed fruits and nuts. It is also customary to eat of the Seven Species: wheat, barley, grapes, figs, pomegranates, olives, and dates.

Ta'anit Esther

Ta'anit Esther is a minor fast day traditionally held on Purim Eve. This holiday cannot be observed on Shabbat. The observance date may be moved to not conflict with Shabbat. Like the other minor fast days, it is customary to fast from dawn until three stars appear in the sky, and those who are ill (even if the condition is not life-threatening) and pregnant or nursing women do not need to fast. I read somewhere this fast, if completed, will make up for any meals said without a blessing.

This fast is often said to commemorate the three-day fast observed by Esther, Mordechai, and the Jewish people before Queen Esther went to plead for the Jewish people who were to be eradicated by Haman.

However, interestingly, this three day fast would have originally occurred during the month of Nisan (specifically during Passover) during which fasting is generally prohibited. In the book of Esther, it mentions a second fast on Adar 13 which was observed by all of Israel as they prepared to fight Haman and his army.

Purim

If Sukkot and its immediately following holidays did not confuse you, I bring you Purim. Before I get into what Purim is, I feel the need to explain that Purim is... odd. This is partially due to the month it falls in, which doubles during leap years. Yes, Judaism is so odd that it inserts an entire month, not just a day! So instead of the month of Adar, during a leap year we have Adar I and Adar II, which both have a version of Purim! To add to this, Purim is celebrated on different days in different cities, and if Purim falls on Shabbat it turns into a three-day festival.

Let's start with the fact Purim takes place on different dates. In non-walled cities, it takes place on the 14th day of Adar. In walled cities (or cities that were walled during the time of Joshua), it takes place on the 15th day of Adar because Jews in walled cities, like Shushan, fought on Adar 13 and Adar 14 and rested on Adar 15, while the Jews in unwalled cities fought on Adar 13 and rested on Adar 14. This comes from a passage in the Book of Esther:

> "But the Jews in Shushan mustered on both the 13th and 14th days and so rested on the 15th and made it a day of feasting and merrymaking. That is why village Jews who live in unwalled towns observe the 14th day of the month Adar and make it a day merrymaking and feasting and as a holiday and an occasion for sending gifts to one another" (Esther 9:18-19).

Further, if you remember, the Hebrew calendar has leap years where an entire month gets added to the calendar. Adar is the repeated month, so during a leap year there is Adar I and Adar II. In this case, Purim is celebrated on the appropriate date during Adar II. During Adar I, however, the dates are marked by holidays called Purim Katan (Little Purim) or Shushan Purim Katan. These are treated as minor holidays and as a reminder of the main Purim holiday coming up.

For those who are in a walled city when Shushan Purim occurs on a Shabbat, it turns into a three-day holiday called Purim Meshulash.[7] During Purim Meshulash celebrations, the mitzvot are split so they do not interfere with Shabbat. The scroll of Esther readings and giving tzedakah to the poor occur on Purim dePrazos (Adar 14) while giving food to friends and the celebratory meal occur on Adar 16.

Now we can discuss what Purim is all about. In the book of Esther, the scroll that is read twice on Purim, a young Jewish woman, Esther, who was hiding her faith, won a beauty contest and became the new queen. Esther's cousin Mordechai, who raised her, remains near the

---

[7]   The calendar does not allow for Adar 14 to fall on Shabbat.

palace. Mordechai learns about a plot to kill the king, reports it to Esther, and his service is recorded.

Not long after, the king appoints evil Haman as Prime Minister. Haman does not like Mordechai because Mordechai does not bow to him. Haman complains to the king and is given permission to kill all the Jews. Mordechai learns of this and tells Esther, who then seeks an audience with the king and asks him to attend a banquet with Haman, then asks for another feast later.

Haman is still annoyed by Mordechai's refusal to bow and wants to hang him the next day. The king suffers from insomnia and has the court records read to him to help him fall asleep and, when reminded of Mordechai's service, learns nothing was done to honor him. Haman, missing part of the conversation and thinking the king wanted him honored, suggests anyone the king wishes to honor should be dressed in the king's royal robes and led around on the king's horse.

Haman is ordered to do so to Mordechai. During the second banquet, Esther tells the king she is Jewish and tells him of Haman's plans to exterminate the Jewish people. The king orders Haman hung on the gallows. Since the previous royal decree allowing the Jews to be killed could not be overturned, another decree was issued allowing the Jewish people to defend themselves and kill anyone who posed a threat.

Over 75,000 enemies are killed, including all ten of Haman's sons. Mordechai is given a royal appointment and issues a decree calling for the holiday of Purim to be celebrated annually. It is custom, when the scroll summarizing this tale is read, to make a lot of noise every time Haman's name is uttered.

Besides listening to the scroll read twice, charity is given to the poor. Another mitzvot includes giving ready to eat packages of food to friends and family. Further, a large celebratory meal is held and all those who can drink alcohol (the ill, the young, or those in recovery from alcoholism do not have to drink) are commanded to drink until they cannot tell the difference between Mordechai and Haman. Many congregations put on a Purim spiel (play) that retells the story of Purim. Cross-dressing, festive dress, and costumes are also very common around Purim time.

Rosh Chodesh Nisan

This is one of the Jewish New Years, specifically for the counting of the reigns of kings. It is relatively arbitrary and, as it was explained to me by a rabbi at Chabad, similar to a company's fiscal year. There is no particular observance for this day. Since I mentioned four Jewish New Years, I felt all of them should be mentioned.

Ta'anit Bechorot

This is a minor fast day prior to Passover that commemorates the salvation of the Israelite firstborns during the plague of the firstborn. As this is also minor fast day, the rules about who may fast are more lenient. The ill (even if the condition is not life-threatening) should not fast.

There is a question over who should fast. Traditionally it is male first-borns who fast, although female first-borns were also saved, so some communities will also have women fast as well as men. Parents may also be advised to fast until their first born is of religious adulthood. It is recommended to consult a rabbi if you have any questions. There is also a dispute as to when to end the fast due to the presence of Passover although all agree the fast starts at dawn. In order to handle this dispute, many communities finish a tract of Torah study so that the community can have a festival meal allowing the first-borns to break their fast early.

Pesach / Passover

As Passover is mostly referred to as Passover rather than Pesach among most English-speaking Jews, I am going to continue to write it as Passover. Passover is two holidays combined into one.

The first holiday is Passover, when HaShem passed over the Israelite houses during the tenth plague. The second holiday is the Feast of Unleavened Bread (Chag HaMatzot) when the Israelites were fleeing from the Egyptians. In total, it lasts for seven days in Israel and the

Reform Jews in Diaspora and eight days among more traditional Jews in Diaspora. Like Sukkot, it is one of the three pilgrimage festivals when Jews were expected to go to Jerusalem and offer a sacrifice.

This holiday is celebrated by having one or two seders (depending on if you are in Israel or Diaspora). The seder is an enormously complex meal including the retelling of the story of the Exodus. Additionally, Jews observing Passover will alter their diet to avoid leavened products and will remove these items from their home.

There may be a ritual involving looking for leavened products throughout the home and then burning them. Frequently, Jews will temporarily sell their bread to Gentiles during this week so they can avoid being in possession of them. While during Passover it is possible to eat products made from the five major grains (wheat, rye, barley, oats and spelt), the food item would need to be completely prepared and cooked within eighteen minutes so as to cook it before it rises. Further, it is a common Ashkenazi minhag to avoid rice, corn, and legumes (such as peanuts and beans) as well during Passover.

Counting of the Omer and Lag B'Omer

The Counting of the Omer starts on the second day of Passover (Nisan 16) and lasts for forty-nine days. Each day, a special blessing is given and many Jews take this time for self-reflection. This period also has partial mourning restrictions and weddings, parties, dancing, and haircuts are all prohibited.

This is due to a massive plague that killed thousands. These mourning restrictions are lifted on Lag B'Omer, representing a break in the plague. Others, particularly students of Kabbalah, celebrate this as a Kabbalistic holiday.

On Lag B'Omer, all mourning restrictions are lifted and it is treated as a minor holiday. Weddings are permitted. Bonfires and parades are common. It is also a day that is often used to give a child, generally a son, their first haircut.

Israeli Holidays—Yom HaShoah, Yom HaZikaron, Yom HaAtzma'ut and Yom Yerushalayim

The following holidays were signed into law by the state of Israel. In the Diaspora, they may or may not be celebrated and if they are celebrated, the customs may be different depending on the congregation.

Yom HaShoah is also known as Holocaust Remembrance Day. This falls on the 27th of Nisan unless this day is adjacent to Shabbat, in which case Yom HaShoah is moved by a day. This is a time where we recognize the approximately six million Jews who were killed during the Holocaust. Often special prayers, as well as Kaddish, are said, and it is also a frequent period of Holocaust education and lectures.

Yom HaZikaron is Israeli Memorial Day, but it also has a deeper meaning. The official name is the Day of Remembrance for Israeli Fallen Soldiers and Victims of Terrorism. On this day, the Israeli flag flies at half mast and sirens blow periodically for a minute of silence. Cars will even stop on the highway in order to observe the minute of silence. Yom HaZikaron is always the day before Yom HaAtzma'ut and is usually celebrated on Lyar 4 although the date can vary depending on if Lyar 5 falls on Friday or Saturday.

Yom HaAtzma'ut is Israeli Independence Day and is celebrated similarly to how July 4th is celebrated in America, with lots of special events, BBQ, picnics, and fireworks. It is usually Lyar 5, but it can vary as it may not occur on Friday or Saturday.

Yom Yerushalayim is Jerusalem Day, a minor holiday celebrating the reunification of Jerusalem after the Six Day War and is celebrated on Lyar 28.

Shavuot

Immediately after the Counting of the Omer, comes the holiday of Shavuot. During Shavuot, we are reminded of the giving of the Torah to the Jewish people at the base of Mount Sinai. Shavuot lasts for one day in Israel and two days in Diaspora. It is also a pilgrimage festival when Jews were expected to go to Jerusalem.

This holiday is celebrated by reading the Book of Ruth, staying up all night in Torah study, and by eating at least one dairy meal, which earned it the nickname the "Cheesecake Holiday." Followers of Kabbalah often have a tradition that at exactly midnight on Shavuot to go outside and look for G-d. Shavuot also contains the reading of Ruth's story, which as Jews by Choice, we all will experience. In some congregations, Jews by Choice are particularly honored on this holiday.

Personally, this is one of my favorite holidays. As an eternal student, I am used to staying up all night studying one subject or another, so the main difference for me is the cheesecake!

The Weeks of Mourning from Tzom Tammuz to Tisha B'Av

The last major holiday before we start preparing for the high holy days is one of the saddest periods of the Jewish calendar where we commemorate the destruction of the First and Second Temples and exile from Israel. The mourning intensifies and each period has different rituals.

The Three Weeks of Mourning start on the 17th day of Tammuz which is a minor fast day. Like other minor fast days, it is customary to fast from dawn until three stars appear in the sky and this holiday cannot be observed on Shabbat.

This fast commemorates the breaking of the first set of ten commandments, the breach of Jerusalem's walls by the Romans, Jews ceasing to offer sacrifices, the burning of a Torah scroll, and the erection of an idol in the Temple, among others.

It is the beginning of one of the most depressing parts of the Jewish calendar. The customs of Ashkenazi Jews during the Three Weeks of Mourning include refraining from haircuts, avoiding joyous occasions, listening to music, or watching other public entertainment.

Ashkenazi Jews during the final Nine Days (starting at the beginning of Av), will intensify their mourning by avoiding poultry, red meat, wearing freshly cleaned clothing (except on Shabbat for adults, babies are always exempt and may always have clean clothing) and from taking warm showers and baths (babies and young children are also exempt).

On Tisha B'Av, a major fast day like Yom Kippur, during services, the congregants traditionally sit on low stools as when sitting Shiva. This fast day commemorates the destruction of both Temples and some movements also recognize Holocaust victims on this day. An interesting custom among Ashkenazi Jews is to wear tefillin and tallit gadol at the afternoon service rather than at morning prayers.

Rosh Chodesh Elul

This is one of the Jewish New Years, specifically for the counting of animal tithes. It should be noted some Talmudic sources put this on the same day as Rosh Hashanah. While there is no particular observance for this day, I felt all Jewish New Years should be mentioned.

Hebrew Name	English Name	Date	Meaning	Mitzvot/ Customs	Feast or Fast
Shabbat	Sabbath	Every week, starting Friday at sunset and lasting 25 hours	Day of Rest	Observing Shabbat Enjoying Shabbat Sanctifying Shabbat Resting Refraining from work	Feast (3 festive meals)
Rosh Hashanah	Head of New Year	Tishrei 1 and 2	Day of Judgment	Hearing the shofar Praying in the synagogue Refraining from work Personal Reflection	Feast (festive meal to include apples, honey, and round challah)
Tzom Gedaliah	Fast of Gedaliah or Fast of the Seventh Month	Tishrei 3	Fast of Gedaliah	Fast from dawn until three stars appear in the sky Personal Reflection	Fast
Yamim Noraim	Days of Awe or Days of Repentance	Tishrei 1 through Tishrei 10	Days of Repentance	Personal Reflection	Depends on the day. See Rosh Hashanah, Tzom Gedaliah, Yom Kippur
Yom Kippur	Day of Atonement	Tishrei 10	Day of Atonement	Fast (25 hour) Personal Reflection Refraining from work	Fast

Hebrew Name	English Name	Date	Meaning	Mitzvot/ Customs	Feast or Fast
Sukkot	Feast of Booths or Feast of Tabernacles	Tishrei 15 through Tishrei 21 (Tishrei 22 in Diaspora)	Feast of Booths, Season of our Rejoicing, Festival of Ingathering	Refrain from work (first two days) Eating in a sukkah Waving branches (lulav) and a fruit (etrog) during services	Feast
Shemini Atzeret	Eighth day of Assembly	Tishrei 22 (in Israel), Tishrei 22 and 23 (in Diaspora)	Eighth day of Assembly	Prayer for Rain Refrain from work	Feast
Simchat Torah	Rejoicing with/of the Torah	Tishrei 22 in Israel, Tishrei 23 in Diaspora	Rejoicing with/of the Torah	Aliyah for as many as possible Torah Procession Refrain from work	Normal
Hanukkah	Festival of Lights	Kislev 25 through Tevet 2 (or Tevet 3 depending on how many days are in Kislev)	Festival of rededication	Candle-lighting	Normal (although fried foods are common)
Asara B'Tevet	Fast of the Tenth of Tevet	Tevet 10	Fast of the Tenth of Tevet	Fast from dawn until three stars appear in the sky	Fast
Tu B'Shevat (or Ḥamisha Asar BiShvat)	Jewish Arbor Day	Shevat 15	New Year of Trees	Tu B'Shevat Seder Tree Planting	Feast (of fruits)

Hebrew Name	English Name	Date	Meaning	Mitzvot/ Customs	Feast or Fast
Purim Katan	Little Purim	Adar I, 14th in leap years	Little Purim	No specific observance, custom to have special meal	Feast
Shushan Purim Katan (In walled cities may just called Purim Katan.)	Little Shushan Purim (for walled cities). In walled cities may just called Purim Katan.	Adar I, 15th in leap years	Little Shushan Purim	No specific observance but treated as a minor holiday, custom to have special meal	Feast
Ta'anit Esther	Fast of Esther	Adar 13 in most years, Adar 11 if Adar 13 should fall on Shabbat. In leap years, this is held during the second month of Adar	Fast of Esther	Fast from dawn until three stars appear in the sky Tzedakah to the poor	Fast
Purim	Purim	Adar 14 in Diaspora. In leap years, this is held during the second month of Adar	Purim	Scroll of Esther Giving food to friends Giving tzedakah to poor Celebratory meal	Feast
Purim de-Prazos (only called this in walled cities)	Purim de-Prazos (only called this in walled cities)	Adar 14 in walled cities. In leap years, this is held during the second month of Adar.	Purim de-Prazos (only called this in walled cities)	During Purim Meshulash celebrations, Scroll of Esther Giving tzedakah to poor	Feast

Hebrew Name	English Name	Date	Meaning	Mitzvot/ Customs	Feast or Fast
Shushan Purim (simply called Purim in walled cities)	Shushan Purim (simply called Purim in walled cities)	Adar 15 in walled cities. In leap years, this is held during the second month of Adar	Shushan Purim (simply called Purim in walled cities)	Scroll of Esther Giving food to friends Giving tzedakah to poor Celebratory meal If on Shabbat, mitzvot are moved to other days	Feast
Purim Meshulash	Three-fold Purim	Adar 14 through Adar 16 in walled cities when Shushan Purim falls on Shabbat. This name also refers to Adar 16 during this time	Third day of Purim	During Purim Meshulash, Giving food to friends Celebratory meal	Feast
Rosh Chodesh Nisan	First of Nisan / New Year for Kings	Nisan 1	First of Nisan / New Year for Kings	King's reign is advanced by a year	Normal
Ta'anit Bechorot	Fast of the First Born	Nisan 14, unless Passover begins on a Sunday then it is Nisan 12	Fast of the First Born	Fast from dawn, usually broken several hours later at a celebratory meal commemorating the end of a study of a tract of Torah	Fast

Hebrew Name	English Name	Date	Meaning	Mitzvot/ Customs	Feast or Fast
Pesach / Chag HaMatzot	Passover / Feast of Unleavened Bread	Nisan 15 through Nisan 21 (in Israel and among Diaspora Reform Jews) or Nisan 22 (in traditional Diaspora)	Passover / Feast of Unleavened Bread	One or two seders Passover sacrifice (during times of the Temple) Cannot eat leavened bread	Feast
Sefirat Ha'omer	Counting of the Omer	16 Nisan—5 Sivan	Counting the days from the second day of Pesach to Shavout	Special prayers Time of partial mourning	Normal
Yom HaShoah	Holocaust Remembrance Day	27th of Nisan unless this day is ad-jacent to Shabbat	Holocaust Remembrance Day	Special prayers Kaddish Holocaust education	Normal
Yom HaZikaron	Day of Remembrance for Israeli Fallen Soldiers and Victims of Terrorism	Varies de-pending on if Lyar 5 falls on Friday or Saturday, it is always the day before Yom HaAtzma'ut. Usually Lyar 4	Memorial Day	Special memorial service Sirens Israeli flag at half staff	Normal
Yom HaAtzma'ut	Israeli Independence Day	Varies de-pending on if Lyar 5 falls on Friday or Saturday, it is always the day after Yom HaZikaron, Usually Lyar 5	Independence Day	Special prayers Special events	Either Normal, Fast, or Feast. Fast is the rarest.

Hebrew Name	English Name	Date	Meaning	Mitzvot/Customs	Feast or Fast
Lag B'Omer	33rd day of the Omer	Lyar 18	33rd day of the Omer	Mourning restrictions removed	Normal or Feast
Yom Yerushalayim	Jerusalem Day	Lyar 28	Jerusalem Day	Special prayers Special events Festive meals	Feast
Shavuot	Festival of Weeks	Sivan 6 (in Diaspora Sivan 6 and Sivan 7)	Festival of Weeks Festival of the Giving of Our Torah	Festive meals All night Torah study Book of Ruth Work not permitted	Feast (dairy)
Tzom Tammuz	Fast of Seventeenth of Tammuz	Seventeenth of Tammuz	Fast of Seventeenth of Tammuz	Fast from dawn until three stars Special prayers	Fast
Bein ha-Metzarim	Three Weeks of Mourning	Tammuz 17 through Av 9	Three Weeks of Mourning	Special haftorot Increased mourning No haircuts, no weddings, no joyous occasions, no music	Normal or Fast depending on the day
Tisha B'Av	9th of Av	Av 9	9th of Av	Special haftarot Fast Customs same as Yom Kippur Torah draped in black Additional mourning restrictions Different minhagim	Fast

Hebrew Name	English Name	Date	Meaning	Mitzvot/ Customs	Feast or Fast
Rosh Chodesh Elul	First of Elul/ New Year for Animals	Elul 1 (note some sources place this on Tishrei 1)	First of Elul/ New Year for Animals	Currently none Previously one of every ten cattle was sacrificed	Normal

APPENDIX B

SAMPLE CONVERSION ESSAY

The longer I live and the more I learn, the more I realize it has long been my fate to join the Jewish people. I was born and raised in South Florida, which has a rather vibrant Jewish community so, like many Gentiles there, I was raised interfaith despite being born to two Roman Catholic parents.

With such a significant amount of the population being Jewish, you grow up surrounded by Jewish culture, Jewish knowledge, and get a basic Jewish education. As one person said over Pesach, you become Jewish by proxy. My joke was if you weren't born to a Jewish mother, you were still assigned one at birth.

I know the Roman Catholic Church didn't appreciate the Jewish influence, particularly the question-asking aspect. Catholics already did not appreciate my gender-nonconforming behavior (I bucked gender roles as a very tomboyish girl), but the final straw was my never-ending questioning of every aspect of religious life. I was threatened with excommunication at age eight and told never to return. I was happy about this, because I knew this meant I would be free to find my own path.

I knew a few things at this point. One, there was a higher power. Two, any faith I followed had to allow questions. Three, any religion that followed the New Testament was not my religion. Jesus was... at best... a carpenter and since we are all G-d's children, he was no more or less the son of G-d than I was.

I knew Judaism met the basic criteria, and I certainly knew I fit in better with the surrounding Jewish community than the Catholic one.

Since I did not want to simply assume Judaism was my definite home, I looked for a better match.[8] I read about many religions and the closest match remained Judaism.

The only problem was, as far as my reading and the people I spoke to said, Judaism was not a religion you could convert to. You could be born to it, but you couldn't join it. As far as I understood it, Ruth seemed to be the only convert in Jewish history. This made me sad, as the religion seemed right for me and was certainly a better fit than I originally imagined.

I was able to keep my favorite Biblical stories, I didn't need an intermediary to talk to G-d, I respected rabbis' role in the community (much different than a Catholic priest's), no real "Hell" to speak of, the holidays and traditions felt right to me, the Jewish version of G-d was very loving and seemed so unlike the Christian counterpart, plus this was more than a religion and more like a way of life. Plus I was so at home in the culture, some Jewish friends joked that my Gentile parents stole a Jewish baby.

As a teenager, I started dating. In the Jewish community I was originally in (mostly Miami), all the parents told their sons that I was off-limits, and I respected that. I went to magnet high school about an hour away and seemed to attract every Jewish boy in the school. I have no idea why.

There were a lot of racial issues and a lot of antisemitism, so dating options for Jewish students were limited. I just cared that I was being asked out by smart, nice, good-looking guys who appreciated my intelligence and love of education. The fact we had other similarities and values (an interest in charity, being generally liberal, tending to fight for the rights of the underprivileged, etc) also may have played a role.

I made my non-Jewish status clear right after I was asked out, since I knew this was a different community where my parents were not known. No one really cared. One of the guys I dated was very observant

---

[8]   While it might sound odd that a child was on a spiritual quest, this seems to be a family tradition. My mother became Roman Catholic at 7 and I will be a fifth generation convert, possibly sixth, on the matrilineal line.

(he identified as Conservadox), and he wanted to eventually live a more Orthodox lifestyle.

He was the one who told me that there have been other conversions besides Ruth and that conversion occurred even today. He was frequently asked to help participate in or co-teach conversion courses, so he was very familiar with the process. Like so many of my friends, I thought it was only possible to be Jewish if you had a Jewish mother (or if you were Reform, father).

I said I wanted to learn more and maybe consider conversion down the line. Everyone else was already considering me as close to being Jewish as you could be without actually being Jewish, many of my beliefs were already in line with Jewish teachings and values, and I had a somewhat Jewish identity, so wanting more intensive study wasn't a difficult decision to make.

I am not entirely sure what happened, but I do know within a matter of weeks I was getting tutored three to four hours a day, four or five days a week, for about eight or so months. There were a few tutors, all following a curriculum given by a Conservative rabbi (actually one of my boyfriend's rabbis). I had even more hours per day during summertime when secular school was out.

I originally thought the weekly hours were excessive but then met high school classmates of mine who were trying to convert. One friend had ten to fifteen hours a week, and she wanted to convert to Reform. Another friend who converted Orthodox put my hours to shame. She told me about a year ago that she suspected our curriculums were so much more intense just because we were teens who were raised in a Jewish area, so rabbis expected more from us. Not only that, but antisemitism was on the rise, so this was a way to assure we knew what we were getting into.

The fact is, I loved every minute of studying, and I loved gradually including more Judaism into my life. The more of a Jewish life I lived, the more content with the spiritual aspect of my life I was. That boyfriend and I broke up well over a decade ago, but I have kept so many memories and maintained several practices even when it would have been more convenient to drop them.

This isn't to say that it has been a piece of cake trying to convert because it hasn't. I have had more than a few challenges that I have had to overcome in the past sixteen years since I first decided to pursue conversion.

My father really did not take it well years ago, and for my own sanity I have decided not to tell him this time. My mother, who was supportive when I was a teenager, is not taking this well now.[9] My maternal grandmother, who was my strongest supporter years ago, screamed at me for ten minutes before she decided I was an adult. Then she gave me $100 toward my conversion course as her final Christmas gift to me.

I have been with my partner for thirteen years and have been arguing over Jewish practices all this time. I usually win, with the exception of the year-round Christmas tree in the basement. He knows to expect a mezuzah placed opposite the tree. The most important thing for me was "winning" the fight regarding keeping a biblically kosher kitchen. My step-daughter, on the other hand, seems supportive and is very interested in learning more about Judaism herself.

One of the biggest challenges has been the fact I am transgender. When I was trying to convert as a teenager, I approached a rabbi five times, the same rabbi whose curriculum we followed. By the fifth time I was rejected, my Conservadox boyfriend asked what the rationale was since he had only heard of people needing to approach three times.

The rabbi told him that I was too butch as a woman, stated I was probably a lesbian, and that meant I was going to be a bad Jew. The best I could ever hope to be was a righteous Gentile/Noahide and probably not even that. This hurt, and I gave up. As far as I was concerned, this was evidence that HaShem hated me. I was already being rejected and

---

[9]   I am quite certain it is because of Mom's fallout with her best friend who is Jewish. Her friend had several issues with my mother over a short period of time. She was more supportive of me when my mother was dealing with my transgender issues and I sided with her when she was in mourning. She lost her husband and at least one of her parents in a short period of time. My mother did not understand Jewish mourning so didn't understand why her friend really had no interest in doing anything or going anywhere.

insulted by many of my classmates for the same reason, so what is one more person hating me?

It seemed HaShem was just like his Christian counterpart and not as loving as I thought. It took me years to fix the emotional damage and realize I am as HaShem made me. I really was loved, but I simply had a different collection of challenges, including the fact I have epilepsy and Asperger's Syndrome, that others did not.

It was not until I accepted this lesson completely, and accepted myself completely as a transsexual, that I could even begin to try again. I am also still in the process of learning to have full faith in HaShem that He will pull me through and put me where I need to be. Given how poor my life has been lately with the challenges I face, it can be difficult to have faith.

Of course with every journey, there are highlights. I learned there is definitely something fundamentally different about my soul. I have had too many strange coincidences to suggest otherwise. I have had both Gentiles (strangers and friends) and Jews make comments that I seem to have a Jewish soul.

When I was a child, I thought the comments were made in jest, but these seemed more serious. Then it dawned on me that I cannot remember what it was like to live as a Gentile. I do not know how it snuck up upon me. I am not sure exactly when during this journey I went from being the Gentile among Jews to being a Jew among Gentiles.

I sometimes wonder what it means that even though I wanted to convert as a child, I needed to distance myself for years before I came back again. Perhaps this was my way of following this famous quotation: "If you love something, let it go. If it comes back to you, it's yours forever. If it doesn't, then it was never meant to be." I had my chance to live as a Gentile, but I chose to live a more Jewish life.

There are things I learned along the way, although it has been years since I have learned a lot in the academic knowledge department. My worst area knowledge-wise is prayer and service (it would probably work better if I understood Hebrew) despite the fact I listen to many services. I am now taking a Webyeshiva course that will help correct part of that deficiency.

Most of my other knowledge areas are reasonably strong with my strongest being kashrut. Kashrut was particularly important because I kept dating chefs, and my family was always feeding people of different cultures. I also was on medically prescribed diets, which a kosher diet helps me follow. For a person who eats as little as I do, I seem to be obsessed with anything involving food from kashrut to blessings, although I never can remember the blessings so have to look up the transliterated words every time or simply do it in English.

My favorite holidays include Tu B'Shevat, Purim, and Shabbat. I think my love for Shabbat is more because I am so busy during the week that it is nice to have a day where I either do not work at all or do not work as much, plus I have great memories of quality time with my grandmother, which always started Friday night and lasted until Saturday night or early Sunday.

Plus any day that I have the excuse to eat challah makes me happy, as challah is my Achilles' Heel. My maternal grandmother, originally from Long Island, further insists that I have to learn to make gefilte fish despite the fact I hate gefilte fish. I am an environmentalist so I feel a connection to Tu B'Shevat, and I might want to host the Tu B'Shevat seder for next year.

The only thing that would make love Purim more is if I were allowed to drink! I love the entire story and all the mitzvot required, although with how badly I butchered some of the names in the Megillah when I was doing a Skype reading, I think I might want to leave the performance to the professionals. And I love the idea of tzedakah since charity and volunteering has always been a way of life for me.

As for what is next for me, I have several things I want to do. I really would like to study more mysticism / Jewish Renewal. I need to study Hebrew, because I feel like I have to and Yiddish because I want to get my Yiddish understanding back to where it was a few decades ago. I just started volunteering with The Jewish Encounter and, if all goes well, I will be visiting Israel within the next year.

APPENDIX C

RITUAL ITEMS TO CONSIDER PURCHASING

While there is no rule that states you have to purchase all or really any item on this list, this list is provided to you as a reference of items that you might want to purchase as you continue to live Jewishly. Some of these are holiday specific and others are worn on a weekly or daily basis depending on your movement.

A few items are exclusively used by men in some movements, while others are also used by women in more liberal movements. Out of respect to all movements, I am grouping them together by traditional frequency of use. Please confirm with your rabbi regarding your community's standards. Also remember ritual items should be as beautiful as possible.

Frequently Used Items

Handwashing cup—this often two handled cup performs the function that the name implies. Traditional Jews will wash their hands ritualistically upon waking in the morning, after using the restroom, upon leaving a cemetery, and before touching bread. If the cup has two handles, this makes it easier to transfer the cup between the right and left hand.

Cost: $10 and up.

Kippah (or yarmulke)—This is the head covering, more commonly known by the Yiddish name yarmulke. Traditionally worn by men, it is a reminder that we are always in the presence of G-d. Depending on the customs of the community, or your sponsoring denomination, you may wear one all the time or just in services. It is becoming more common for both men and women in more liberal congregations to wear them.

Cost: I purchased one for less than three dollars and I had two given to me. Go to enough Jewish events and you will simply be handed a free kippah. If you travel to Israel, you can get some beautiful kippot in the markets between 10 and 20 shekels (roughly $3 to $6).

Mezuzah—The mezuzah case is a small receptacle affixed to the door-post of a Jewish home, this contains a mezuzah parchment on which the Shema and two passages of Deuteronomy are written. Traditionally, it would not only be affixed to the outside doors but also to most of the doorposts on the inside of the house. It would not be affixed to closets, bathrooms, rooms that are considered too small (I was told the minimum size is 6 foot by 6 foot, but you might want to consult your rabbi), or entrances without proper doorways.

The mezuzah case, with the scroll inside, is affixed on the right side of the doorpost on an angle. Many Jews either kiss the mezuzah case (either directly or indirectly) upon passing one. If you are going to invest money into a mezuzah, it is important to invest the most money into the beauty of the mezuzah scroll itself as opposed to the mezuzah case. The scrolls are considered either kosher or non-kosher. A kosher scroll will be written by a specially trained scribe on parchment made from the skin of a kosher animal and will have no errors. Every few years, kosher mezuzah scrolls should be checked by a trained scribe in order to assure they are still kosher.

Cost: Mezuzah cases can be found for as little as $10 and there are also creative ways online to learn how to create your own mezuzah case. The mezuzah scrolls are much more expensive and a "kosher" scroll can easily cost $40 although if you are lucky, you can find them for $20, but be sure you get their kosher certificate to assure they are kosher. I was advised by one of my beit din members to consider using non-kosher scrolls which can be purchased for $5 and upgrading the scrolls when I can afford it. However, considering I am more traditional, I have a difficult time justifying the non-kosher scrolls.

Tallit (also pronounced tallis in Ashkenazi pronunciation)—There are two forms of tallit, the tallit gadol and the tallit katan.

The tallit gadol (large tallit) is the prayer shawl worn by adult men in more traditional communities and by both men and women (if they so choose) in more liberal movements. This will be worn daily during morning prayers as a biblical commandment, although there are some exceptions to this rule.

Before donning the tallit, the fringes (tzitzit) should be inspected to assure there is no damage. In some conversion ceremonies, the rabbi will include a time where a tallit is presented to the new Jew. Choosing a tallit can be a very personal experience especially if you are in a more liberal community. Tallitot can be made of silk, wool, or cotton, although wool is more common in the traditional movements.

There are many different sizes, which are partially based on the requirements of your movement and your height. Further, you may also get embroidery or scenes designed into the tallit, although simply having either blue or black stripes is more traditional. I wanted two, one more traditional and one more contemporary. I was lucky enough to be given a gorgeous contemporary shawl style silk tallit by my grandmother and then was given a large black striped tallit by a classmate of mine. If you purchase a tallit gadol, I would also recommend purchasing a tallit bag (for storing it when not in use) and tallit clips especially if you purchase a more traditional tallit gadol.

Cost: $18 and up, although the average price I've seen has been around $50 or more for a traditional tallit. My most expensive tallit, a large one with purple stripes, was about $130. The costs vary depending on size, material, where it has been purchased from, etc. You can get a good deal if you are willing to shop around. My 100% silk tallit was approximately $30 and was imported from Israel. Tallit bags can be found for as little as $5 and tallit clips can be found for as little as $10.

The tallit katan (small tallit), is, as the translation suggests, a small version. It is also simply called tzitzit. This is often worn underneath one's clothes and the tzitzit fringes may or may not be visible. It is similar in design to a poncho and there is an opening for the head and for the arms. If you have ever seen the movie "Fiddler on the Roof," Tevye references this under his clothing.

Cost: Between $10 and $20 on average, this is mostly depending on size and materials. I have seen much more expensive ones as well.

Tefillin—Like the tallit, this is a biblically mandated mitzvah, however I only know a few liberal Jews who do this on a regular basis. Tefillin consists of two black leather boxes attached to leather straps made from a kosher animal. Inside each box is a piece of handwritten parchment consisting of verses from Exodus and Deuteronomy.

One box is wrapped around your weaker arm while the other is affixed to the head. For example, if you are right handed, the tefillin would be donned on your left hand. There are differences between how Ashkenazi and Sephardic Jews don tefillin. Please see your rabbi for information on how to don tefillin as I found this difficult to learn without someone being present.

Cost: The least expensive one I found online was approximately $150, and I had to do extensive comparison shopping in order to find it. Realistically, expect to pay no less than $500 if you decide to purchase this item.

Tzedakah box—Every Jew is obligated to donate money (and time) to positive causes. The tzedakah box helps remind us of this obligation. Many Jews will empty their pockets of loose change before Shabbat starts and place it in their household tzedakah box. When it is full, the coins are given to a charity.

I have seen tzedakah boxes appear in all shapes and sizes from gorgeous replications of synagogues in Prague to the simple blue box from the Jewish National Fund. If you wished, you could even make your own simple tzedakah box using instructions found on the internet.

Cost: If you contact the Jewish National Fund (888-JNF-0099), they will send you a free blue box that you return when it is full. The money collected helps plant trees in Israel. Prior to being given a JNF box as part of a conversion gift, I used a simple Ziploc bag.

Shabbat Items

Candlesticks and Candles—One of the ways we bring in Shabbat is by lighting candles about eighteen minutes before sunset. Since there are candles, we must have a place to hold the candles. Since the commandments include "to remember" and "keep" the Sabbath, we light a minimum of two Shabbat candles. Some families might light an additional candle for each child.

Cost: Candlestick holders vary in price depending on how much you wish to spend. You can often also find them for free on recycle websites such as Freecycle or Craigslist. Alternatively, you might not need them at all. Small tealight candles, for example, have frequently served as my Shabbat candles and they are self-contained. You can purchase tealight candles for as little as ten cents a candle although larger, more traditional Shabbat candles are more typically used.

Challah cover—During every Shabbat except for those that fall during Passover, we have challah, which is a special braided bread. Tradition dictates we should cover the bread, only removing the cover right before the blessing is said. The cover is in part to represent the dew which protected the manna before the Israelites gathered it.

Additionally, as the bread is traditionally blessed first on weekdays (any day that is not Shabbat) when the wine is blessed during Kiddush, the cover is said to prevent the challah from becoming embarrassed that it was not blessed first. At the very least, the challah gets covered by a napkin.

Cost: Custom dictates that any ritual item should be made as beautiful as possible and silk is a common fabric for challah covers. Silk challah covers can be found for $25. However, if you are on a budget, paper napkins or fabric napkins can also be used.

Challah board—Many use challah boards, instead of plates, to place the challah on the table. This also can be considered a part of the representation of the dew that covered the ground that the manna fell on before the Israelites gathered it.

Cost: A very basic challah board can be obtained for less than $10. Alternatively you can use paper plates or a nice normal plate to hold the challah.

Challah knife—In order to make Shabbat special, some use a special knife just for cutting challah. I am not a fan of this, as tradition dictates that challah should be torn, however some people wish to cut it. For those who wish to cut it, a large market has come up to fulfill their needs and desires.

Cost: You can purchase a very nice decorated challah knife for $10. You can also spend more if you wish.

Kiddush cup—This is a wine glass specially set aside specifically for making Kiddush over grape juice or wine. In a pinch, you can use any cup or mug.

Cost: Dedicated Kiddush cups can cost as little as $5 depending on materials. My current favorite Kiddush cup is very lovely, colorful and, most importantly, indestructible and cost me a little over $30. The Kiddush cup will be used again for Havdalah and many other times during the Jewish year. I was also given one for my bar mitzvah.

Havdalah

Havdalah Candles—Special braided candles with two wicks are used to mark the end of Shabbat. If you cannot obtain Havdalah candles, it is also permissible to take two normal candles and braid their wicks together in order to perform the ritual.

Cost: Each candle costs about $6, however a candle will last for a long time as the candle is extinguished only a few minutes after lighting. You may also wish to purchase a special candle holder, often found in matching Havdalah sets, to hold the Havdalah candle, although it is unnecessary.

Spice box—In Judaism, it is sometimes said that Jews gain an extra soul on Shabbat. This soul departs as Havdalah is performed, the spices that one blesses and then passes around is said to help the remaining soul recover from the departure of the second soul, thus acting like smelling salts, but for the soul.

Cost: You can get a spice bag for $6 or a spice box for $10 if you shop around, you could even design and make one yourself. The spice mix themselves can be purchased under the name B'somim (or besamim) for $5.

Rosh Hashanah and Yom Kippur

Apple plate and Honey dish—As part of ushering in a sweet new year, apples and bread are frequently dipped in honey. Many people have special dishes for this holiday although it is not really necessary.

Cost: If you want to go all out, I have seen very nice sets starting in the mid-20s. However, you can make your own special plate or use whatever you like.

Shofar—Honestly, you do not need a personal shofar, as if you attend services you will hear the shofar and thus fulfill the mitzvah of hearing the blast. This is not to say you cannot own a shofar if you want as many people own small shofars for personal use or to play music on.

These are generally not the four or six foot or so shofar frequently purchased by synagogues. Many shofars are less than a foot in size. I was informed that a larger shofar is easier to blow than a shorter one.

Cost: The least expensive shofar that I've seen so far has been approximately $30 online and it was 13 inches. You can also get larger or smaller shofars depending on your preference and how good you want your sound quality to be. I was given my own shofar, which is almost as big as I am.

Kittel—A kittel is a simple white pocket-less burial shroud used to bury male Jews, providing simple dress that assures equality for all even in death. If you are converting as an Ashkenazi male which is the likely culture you are going to convert as, the kittel is used more frequently.

An Ashkenazi male will first wear a kittel on his wedding day when he starts his new life together with his partner. He may then choose to wear it again on Yom Kippur if it is minhag (custom) in his community and may even wear it on Rosh Hashanah. Frequently, it is also worn when leading a Passover Seder.

Cost: So far the lowest cost I have found for a kosher kittel made of unblended fabrics is approximately $60 through a discount website. If you do not follow the requirement of only wearing unblended fabrics, the cost can be lower as there are many places that sell cotton/polyester blends for around $40 to $50.

Sukkot

Succah—The succah is the temporary dwelling that we are commanded to dwell in during the holiday of Sukkot. A succah must have at least two and a half walls, but it can be of any size so long as it allows you to dwell and take meals there. The roof must be made of natural material and when the succah is covered, there should be enough space between the natural gaps in order that the stars can be seen. In the event it is raining, a cover can be placed over the roof temporarily, but that invalidates the succah for use to fulfill the mitzvah and should be removed as quickly as possible.

Cost: To be honest, I would strongly recommend building the succah from scratch, because the pre-made succah kits can run into the hundreds of dollars. I am not mechanically inclined, so it is almost worth it to spend $300 or more on a pre-built succah. Most people I know simply purchase materials from Home Depot or Lowe's and build it. There are succah building instructions online. Succah decorations can be very inexpensive as families often have artwork done by the children hanging on the walls.

Etrog Box—When not in use during Sukkot, the etrog fruit often is placed in a decorative box. The box should be as beautiful as possible.

Cost: The cost can be as little as $5 and the prices go up from there. The etrog itself varies in price with the most flawless ones being more expensive.

Lulav Holder—As the name implies, this is the holder for the lulav used during Sukkot.

Cost: The cost can be as little as $5 for a plastic holder.

Hanukkah

Dreidel—This is a gambling game that originally was used to hide the studying of Torah. Originally based on a German game, this is a favorite game of young Ashkenazi Jews around Hanukkah time. The letters have been used as an acronym for *Nes Gadol Hayah Sham* ("A great miracle happened there") or in Israel *Nes Gadol Hayah Poh* ("A great miracle happened here").

The rules of the game are as follows: each player has a pot of items to bet with (often chocolate coins called gelt). If a gimmel is spun (ג), the spinner gets the full pot. If a hei is spun (ה), the spinner gets half the pot. If a nun is spun (נ), nothing happens and if a shin [ש] (or pei [פ]) is spun, you put one in.

Some dreidels will also have the names of the letters written on them for those who do not recognize Hebrew characters. If dreidel is too mainstream or childish for you, there are also variants of dreidel such as No-Limit Texas Dreidel, which is what it sounds like, a cross between Texas Hold'em and dreidel. In full disclosure, I briefly worked for the inventor of the game.

Cost: Cheap plastic dreidels can be purchased for under a dollar. In my opinion, wooden ones spin better. Many people have made a habit of collecting dreidels since some can be rather elaborate.

Menorah (Chanukkiyah)—The Chanukkiyah is the special nine-branched menorah used specifically for Hanukkah. A normal menorah would only have seven. Every day, an additional candle is added such as on the first day, there is one helper candle (raised higher than the rest) and one normal candle, the second has a helper candle and two normal candles, and it continues until the helper candle and the eight normal candles are all lit.

When the candles are placed in the menorah, they are placed from right to left (like Hebrew is read) but when they are lit, they are lit from left to right (like English is read) using the helper candle. On the days when Hanukkah falls on Shabbat, the Hanukkah candles should be lit first in order to prevent kindling a flame after Shabbat has started. In locations where it is dangerous to have an open flame or it is otherwise forbidden, an electric Chanukkiyah can be purchased and used.

Cost: A low cost non-electric menorah can be purchased between $10 and $15 dollars. Electric ones will start in the mid-$20s and go up from there. Special boxes of Hanukkah candles which contain all the candles needed for the holiday can be purchased for as little as $5 and go up from there.

Purim

Grogger—As part of the festival of Purim, there is a reading of the scroll of Esther. During this reading, it is customary to "blot" out the name of Haman with whatever you can. Some people stomp their feet and others use a grogger which is a handheld noise making device. You spin it and it makes noise.

Cost: Plastic groggers can be found very cheaply, although they usually come in a bulk bag, and may even be provided by the congregation. Alternatively, a cheap, but relatively sturdy wooden grogger will cost you about $4. Of course, there are fancier groggers as well.

Passover

The following assumes you are hosting your own Seder. If you are not hosting your own Seder, then these items are unneeded unless you are asked to bring them.

Afikoman bag—During part of the Passover Seder, there is a time when one of the pieces of matzah are broken apart, placed in an afikoman bag, and hidden (either by adults or children depending on the family's custom, with the other group trying to find it or paying to get it back).

This afikoman is eaten at the end of the Seder as it is meant to be dessert. The bag is often beautifully decorated.

Cost: $6 and up or you can make one yourself.

Elijah's cup—As part of the Passover Seder, a special cup for the prophet Elijah is set aside. During the Seder, there is a time when the door is opened to welcome Elijah and invite him to the Seder. From what I understand, the placement of the cup at the table was due to early rabbis trying to decide whether four or five cups of wine should be drunk at the Passover Seder. As Elijah was said to help judge and rule on difficult questions, Elijah is to decide whether or not the fifth cup is to be drunk at the Seder.

Cost: $10 and up.

Matzah cover—During the Passover Seder, the matzah is covered until it is ready to be used. Similar to how challah is covered on Shabbat.

Cost: $6 and up unless you make one yourself.

Miriam's cup—A relatively new addition to the Passover Seder is the placement of Miriam's cup filled with water and set near the Elijah's cup to remind us of Miriam's contribution when the Israelites were escaping Egypt. Wherever Miriam went, the Israelites would have water, as a well seemed to follow Miriam. When she passed away, there was no more water. This is more commonly seen in the more liberal Jewish communities to honor the role of women in Jewish history.

Cost: $10 and up.

Seder plate—During Passover Seder, there is at least one Seder plate where there are spaces for six (some people have seven) symbolic foods which include maror (a bitter herb usually horseradish), chazeret (another herb, often romaine lettuce), charoset (a fruit/nut mixture resembling mortar), karpas (another vegetable usually parsley or celery that is later dipped either in salt water, vinegar, or charoset), zeroa (a roasted shank bone, some vegetarians will instead use a beet), and beitzah (a hardboiled egg).

Some Jews will also include an orange to represent marginalized Jews such as LGBT Jews, although it is very difficult to find a plate that has a place for seven items.

Cost: $7 and up, although the coolest Seder I attended made little Seder plates for everyone in attendance. The only Seder plate I saw when I looked for one that had a place for an orange was $200 or more. I spent a few days acquiring my own materials and I made my own seder plate with seven sections. It cost about $30, most of which was the blank plate itself.

APPENDIX D

ADDITIONAL RESOURCES

Recommended Jewish books

Barnavi, E. and M. Eliav-Feldon (1992). <u>A historical atlas of the Jewish people : from the time of the patriarchs to the present</u>. New York, Knopf : Distributed by Random House.

A great historical atlas.

Dimont, M. I. (1984). <u>The amazing adventures of the Jewish people</u>. New York, Behrman House.

A concise history of the Jewish people in less than 200 pages.

Donin, H. (1991). <u>To be a Jew : a guide to Jewish observance in contemporary life : selected and compiled from the Shulhan arukh and Responsa literature, and providing a rationale for the laws and the traditions</u>. [New York, N.Y.], BasicBooks.

An excellent introduction to how to live a more Orthodox lifestyle.

Frank, A. (1995). <u>The diary of a young girl : the definitive edition</u>. New York, Doubleday.

This is the unabridged version of the classic diary.

Goldstein, Z. (2010). <u>The complete Shabbat table companion</u>. [Satellite Beach, Fla.], The Jewish learning Group.

You name the Shabbat-related blessing and it's in here including blessings for different holidays. It also includes a lot of Shabbat songs, but most are in Hebrew.

Jewish Publication Society. (1999). Tanakh = JPS Hebrew-English Tanakh. Philadelphia, Jewish Publication Society.
You will need a Tanakh. This includes the Torah, Prophets, and Writings. You can get a student edition.

Kolatch, A. J. (1981). The Jewish book of why. Middle Village, NY, J. David Publisher.
I first read this book many many years ago, and it really helped my understanding of Jewish culture. There is also a sequel called the Second Jewish Book of Why.

Kolatch, A. J. (2005). A handbook for the Jewish home. Middle Village, N.Y., Jonathan David Publishers.
An excellent introduction to how to live a Conservative lifestyle.

Kukoff, L. (1981). Choosing Judaism. New York, N.Y., Union of American Hebrew Congregations.
A convert's discussion on how to "own" their Judaism.

Olitzky, K. M. and R. H. Isaacs (1993). The How-To Handbook for Jewish Living. Hoboken, N.J., KTAV Pub. House.
Now this is a real how-to book. This is almost everything you need to know for most Jewish things.

PunkTorah.org (2012). Choosing To Be Chosen: Essays By Converts To Judaism. Atlanta, Georgia, PunkTorah.
Nice little collection of conversion stories to Judaism. This shows everyone's path to HaShem is different, but we all found our way back home to Him.

Telushkin, J. (2008). <u>Jewish literacy : the most important things to know about the Jewish religion, its people, and its history</u>. New York, William Morrow.

By far one of the most extensive compilations of everything you would ever need to know. I consider this a must have for any Jewish library. I would just not recommend reading it straight through, as it is definitely more a reference book than anything!

Washofsky, M. (2001). <u>Jewish living : a guide to contemporary Reform practice</u>. New York, URJ Press.

A guide to Reform Jewish practice and Reform Jewish living.

Recommended Jewish movies

(1955). Night and Fog. France.

This has to be one of the best documentaries on what life was like in the camps. This is not Jewish specific, which always helps given there were about as many Gentiles killed as there were Jews.

(1995). Mysteries of the Bible. Abraham--one man, one God. United States.

Archaeologists, scholars and historians attempt to replicate and investigate the life of Abraham.

(2011). In Heaven Underground: The Weissensee Jewish Cemetery.

This is a documentary about a very old, very large Jewish cemetery in Germany. It is not so much a cemetery as a necropolis.

Amaral, J., C. Atkins, et al. (2010). Hijacking the Holy Land Palestine, propaganda and peace.

The media tends to be lopsided in its portrayal of Israel. This gives an unbiased look.

Brillhart, A., A. Goldberg, et al. (2009). Jerusalem: Center of the World. [Alexandria, Va.], PBS Home Video.

It is what it implies, the entire history of Jerusalem.

Cran, W., R. B. Satloff, et al. (2010). Among the righteous lost stories from the holocaust in Arab lands. United States.

This discussed camps in North Africa and how some Arabs helped to save Jewish lives.

Daum, M. (2001). A Life Apart: Hasidism in America. New York.

This is a documentary that took seven years to make and was recommended very highly to me by Gentiles who did not know I was Jewish. It is a very interesting look at Hasidic Jews.

Daum, M., O. Rudavsky, et al. (2004). Hiding and Seeking: Faith and Tolerance after the Holocaust. [New York, N.Y.], First-Run Features.

A Jewish father journeys with his two ultra-Orthodox sons back to Poland to try to find the Gentiles who hid their family from the Nazis.

Harris, M. J. (2000). Into the Arms of Strangers : Stories of the Kindertransport, Warner Bros.

This documentary focuses on the plight of some 10,000 Jewish children who were saved in the 1930s because they were allowed transportation out of the country.

Hercules, B., C. Pugh, et al. (2007). Forgiving Dr. Mengele. Brooklyn, NY, First Run/Icarus Films.

One of the victims of Dr. Mengele's medical experiments tells her story and how she finds the power to forgive him.

Hertwig, M., J. Moll, et al. (2006). Inheritance.

Monika Hertwig, daughter of Amon Goeth, commandant of the Plaszow Concentration Camp, and meets one of her father's former Jewish maids, Helen, who returned to Europe to take her daughter to meet Monika.

Jewison, N. (1971). Fiddler on the Roof. Santa Monica, CA, MGM Home Entertainment.

Perhaps one of the most famous Jewish movies in the world. Everyone knows this movie.

Kempner, A. (2000). The Life and Times of Hank Greenberg.

This is an excellent documentary of baseball Hall-of-Famer Hank Greenberg as told through archival film footage and interviews with fans, teammates, friends, and family. I was recommended many movies when I was in the process of conversion and despite the fact that I do not like baseball, or sports, I felt this movie was worthwhile to watch.

Marks, D. (2009). Sunday Feature : Yiddish: A story of Survival. England.

A documentary about the decline and resurgence of Yiddish, the mother tongue of many Ashkenazi Jews.

Prager, D. (2003). Israel in a time of terror. [United States].

A documentary showing what it is really like to live in Israel from the point of view of ordinary Israeli citizens.

Sanderson, A., M. Segev, et al. (2010). This Is Sodom. Israel.

If you enjoy comedy like Monty Python and you like religious parodies, you will likely enjoy this. It was a blockbuster in Israel, and it tells the story of Lot. The only problem is the movie is in Hebrew, so you might want subtitles. Also at the time of this writing, it is only available on a region 2 DVD.

Wegener, P. H. (1921). Der Golem, wie er in die Welt kam. Germany.

A silent movie that shows one of the mysterious creatures of Jewish legend, the Golem!

Yacus, E., D. Chang, et al. (2009). The Jewish People: A Story of Survival. [United States], PBS Home Video.

This is the story of Jewish survival. From slavery to the loss of their homeland; from exile to antisemitism; from pogroms to near annihilation in the Holocaust, they managed to endure while so many communities have vanished. Spanning millennia, this history of the Jewish people explores how a small group who started as desert nomads overcame countless obstacles to survive to the present day.

Jewish Organizations

American Jewish Committee, AJC
P.O. Box 705
New York, NY 10150
United States
Phone: 212-751-4000
Fax: 212-891-1492

Anti-Defamation League
605 Third Avenue
New York, NY 10158
United States
Phone: 212.885.7700
Fax: 212.867.0709

Jewish National Fund
JNF National Headquarters
42 East 69th Street
New York, NY 10021
United States
(888) JNF-0099

Orthodox Union
11 Broadway
New York, NY 10004
United States
Phone: 212-563-4000
Fax: 212-564-9058

Society for Humanistic Judaism
28611 W. 12 Mile Road
Farmington Hills, MI 48334
United States
Phone: (248) 478-7610
Fax (248) 478-3159

Union for Reform Judaism
633 Third Avenue
New York, NY 10017
United States
Phone: 212-650-4000

United Synagogue of Conservative Judaism
820 Second Avenue
New York, NY 10017-4504
United States
Phone: 212-533-7800
Fax: 212-353-9439

World Jewish Congress
PO Box 90400
Washington, DC 20090
United States

Other resources

Aish.com : http://www.aish.com/

The world's largest Jewish content website with over 10,000 articles on Jewish subjects.

Artscroll : http://www.artscroll.com

Artscroll has a vast collection of books, audio, software, and Judaica products. Further, they have a large listing of many of the brick and mortar Judaica shops in the United States and elsewhere. It should also be known that the site is shomer Shabbat so it may be a challenge to access until Havdalah.

Chabad : http://www.chabad.org/

Chabad-Lubavitch is a branch of Jewish tradition with its roots in the Hasidic movement in the 1700s. If you ever hear of Hasidic Jews, they are most likely this group although there are other groups. Chabad however is very strongly into Jewish education and I cannot speak highly enough about their Ask a Rabbi section.

iTunes : http://itunes.apple.com/

Although it is far from being specifically Jewish, there are a large amount of podcasts available through iTunes. Some of the past podcasts I've listened to include Daily Kabbalah Lesson, JTS Weekly Torah Commentary Podcast, KOACH—Two Minute Torah, Kol Hadash Humanistic Congregation Podcast, Old Jews Telling Jokes Podcast, and Sounds Like Congregation Beth Torah Podcast.

Webyeshiva : http://webyeshiva.org

Webyeshiva (a project of the Academy for Torah Initiatives and Directions) is an online Orthodox yeshiva offering Torah classes on nearly all Torah and Talmud related subjects. Nearly all of their courses are free. You do not have to be Orthodox to take the courses. I cannot tell you how much this little organization has helped me. As a matter of fact when I went to Israel, I insisted on swinging by the office to say hello! I always recommend Webyeshiva.

You're Not Crazy : http://crazyjewishconvert.blogspot.com/ or http://www.buildingajewishlife.com

Even though this is an Orthodox blog, this is an excellent resource for those who are converting to a more liberal form of Judaism.

GLOSSARY

Afikoman—half a piece of matzah used for dessert at Passover Seder.

Aliyah—there are two meanings for this word. One meaning refers to the blessing before and after the Torah is read. The second refers to moving to live in Israel.

Antisemite—a person who does not like Jews. They suffer from antisemitism.

Ashkenazi Jews—Literally "German Jews." Any Jew of Central or Eastern European descent is considered Ashkenazi. Most of the world's Jewish population is of Ashkenazi descent.

Bar mitzvah—the age at which a boy becomes an adult and is responsible for the performance of the mitzvah. Normally this is marked by the ceremony where he leads part or all of a Shabbat morning service and reads from the Torah. This occurs at age thirteen.

Bat mitzvah—the age at which a girl becomes an adult and is responsible for the performance of the mitzvah. Not all communities and denominations have the same requirements, assuming they allow a ceremony to take place or not. This occurs at age twelve.

Beit Din (or Beis Din in Ashkenazi pronunciation, also spelled Bet Din or Beth Din, plural Batei din)—the translation is house of judgment, effectively a Jewish court. Batei din of various sizes can rule on anything from conversion, to financial matters, to divorces, to murder. A beit din for conversion requires three learned Jews, generally rabbis, although in some congregations lay members also serve on beit din.

Beitzah—hard boiled egg on the Passover Seder plate.

Bima—raised pulpit where the service is conducted.

Bris—Yiddish word referring to brit milah.

Brit milah—the circumcision ceremony welcoming a baby boy into the covenant.

Candle-lighting Blessing—candles are used frequently in this religion. Every Shabbat, a minimum of two candles are lit. The blessing in transliteration is : Baruch atah Adonai Eloheinu Melech ha'olam asher kideshanu b'mitzvotav vitzivanu l'hadlik ner shel Shabbat.

Challah—Special braided bread eaten on Shabbat and Yom Tov.

Chanukkiyah—Nine-branched menorah used specifically for Hanukkah.

Chazeret—one of the bitter herbs eaten at the Passover Seder, often romaine lettuce.

Conservadox—a synagogue affiliated with the Conservative moment but is considered to be on the border of Orthodox and Conservative in practice.

Conservative Judaism—A somewhat more liberal branch of Judaism than Orthodox Judaism. Halacha is binding as are the 613 mitzvot however it is adaptable to modern life.

Counting of the Omer—period between the second day of Pesach and the holiday of Shavout.

Days of Awe—The days between Tishrei 1 (Rosh Hashanah) through Tishrei 10 (Yom Kippur) and including those days. These are the ten days when personal reflection and making amends with one's fellow man and G-d are particularly important.

Diaspora—Jews living outside the land of Israel.

Dreidel—Four-sided top used in the Hanukkah game of the same name, also called a sevivon in Hebrew.

Etrog—a large lemon like fruit used during Sukkot.

Eretz Israel—the land of Israel. The boundaries are much larger than the current state of Israel.

Eruv—is a ritual enclosure that changes the definition of property for the purposes of carrying items on Shabbat.

Four Species—the etrog, the palm, the willow, and the myrtle used during Sukkot.

G-d—Observant Jews rarely spell out the name of G-d. Replace the dash with an o.

Gelt—Yiddish for money, chocolate gelt (chocolate coins) is often used for playing dreidel.

Gentile—non-Jewish person, this is the politically correct term.

Ger—the translation is stranger, however it is also used to mean a convert to Judaism.

Glatt—Yiddish word meaning "smooth." The term glatt kosher refers to an animal that has not only been killed under the laws of kashrut, but also has had their organs (at a minimum their lungs) inspected in order to assure the animal had no traces of disease that would have killed them.

Goy—non-Jewish person, this term is sometimes used as an insult, although the word itself is not negative. I once referred to myself as a goy around a Jewish friend, and he was quick to point out that I might be a Gentile (which I was at the time), but was certainly NOT a goy!

Goyim—the translation is "the Nations," but this is the reference to more than one goy/Gentile.

Grogger—Purim noise-making device.

Hatafat dam brit—ceremonial circumcision where a drop of blood is shed.

Haggadah—the book used during Passover Seder.

Halacha—Jewish law.

Hamsa—a hand-shaped protective amulet common in Jewish and Islamic cultures. With the fingers pointed upward, the amulet protects against evil. With the fingers pointed downward, the amulet is good luck and success.

HaMotzi—the blessing said over any bread products. This blessing overrides any other food blessing that might be required (and Judaism has blessings upon blessings upon blessings especially over food). If there is bread on the table, just do this one. The blessing in transliteration is : Baruch atah Adonai Eloheinu Melech ha'olam, hamotzi lechem min haaretz.

Hanukkiyah—the nine-branched menorah used for Hanukkah.

HaShem—direct translation... The Name. One of many names for G-d.

Havdalah—ceremony that marks the end of Shabbat.

Hechsher—a symbol placed on a food item which states the food is kosher. Think of it as a trademark for kosher. There are over 600 hechshers in the United States, the largest and most recognized is the Orthodox Union which consists of a U with a circle around it. Generally there will be a letter or word next to it stating allowing you to figure out if it is milk, meat, or parve.

Holocaust—the systematic extermination of approximately six million Jews during the 1940s. Some scholars also include the systematic extermination and forced labor of several more million additional Gentiles, such as the disabled, the Romani, and LGBT people, who were also targeted.

Humanistic Judaism—a movement of Judaism that focuses more on Jewish identity, Jewish culture, and Jewish history.

Jew by Choice—a convert to Judaism.

Jewish Geography—upon any two Jews meeting each other for the first time, it is common to attempt to find out what mutual friends people have in common. Think of this as "6 degrees of Kevin Bacon," but for Jews.

Kabbalah (also spelled Kabala or Cabala)—literally "receiving," it is a school of mystical thought.

Kabbalist—student of Kabbalah.

Kaddish—a prayer used in mourning rituals. This is one of the prayers where a minyan is required.

Kapparot—ceremony performed during the days of Awe where a live chicken is used as atonement for sins. This tends to only be performed by Hasidic Jews.

Karpas—a vegetable, often parsley or celery which is either dipped in salt water (usually Ashkenazi Jews), vinegar (usually Sephardic Jews), or charoset depending on your custom.

Kashrut—Jewish dietary laws.

Kiddush—this can either be a very short one line blessing or a very long blessing over wine in order to sanctify Shabbat and the holidays. The short blessing is also said any time you drink a grape product. The short blessing in transliteration is : Baruch atah Adonai Eloheinu Melech ha'olam borei pri hagafen.

Kippah—head covering, more commonly known by the Yiddish name yarmulke.

Kittel—white robe that serves as a burial shroud for male Jews. It is first worn by male Ashkenazi Jews at their wedding, then during Yom Kippur, and when leading a Passover Seder.

Kol Nidre—beginning prayer which starts Yom Kippur.

Kosher—traditionally referring to foods made in accordance with kashrut or ritual objects made in accordance with Jewish law, this word has further entered into modern slang referring to something being clean or ok.

Ladino—language of Sephardic Jews, it is a blend of Spanish and Hebrew and is also called Judeo-Spanish.

Lag B'Omer—a break in the mourning traditions during the Counting of the Omer.

Lulav—a bound together set of branches made up of a palm branch, two willow branches and three myrtle branches.

Machzor—specialized siddur used for the High Holy Day services, Rosh Hashanah, and Yom Kippur.

Manna—in Exodus 16, this is the substance that fed the Israelites during their wandering in the desert.

Maror—one of the bitter herbs eaten at the Passover Seder, often horseradish.

Matzah—unleavened bread usually eaten during Passover, tastes like a cracker.

Mechitza—a wall or barrier dividing sexes in Orthodox synagogues.

Menorah—Seven-branched candelabrum which is one of the oldest symbols of Judaism. Technically the nine-branched version used for Hanukkah is called a Chanukkiyah.

Mezuzah—The mezuzah case is a small receptacle affixed to the doorpost of a Jewish home, this contains a mezuzah parchment on which the Shema and two passages of Deuteronomy are written. Most people use the phrase mezuzah to refer to the mezuzah case, however this is not accurate. The mezuzah itself is the scroll inside. The plural of mezuzah is mezuzot.

Mikvah (also spelled mikveh)—ritual bath. It has many ritual uses and is a requirement to convert to Judaism.

Minhag—custom.

Minyan—ten Jewish adults required for the performance of certain prayers. Different movements recognize different qualifications to serve on a minyan, such as Orthodox only accept male Orthodox Jews. Other movements allow women to serve in a minyan. I have even seen some allow Gentiles to serve if a Jewish minyan is unavailable.

Mitzvah—commandment. There are 613 total, roughly half have not been in force since the destruction of the Second Temple. The plural of mitzvah is mitzvot.

Mohel—ritual circumciser. Plural is mohelim.

Noahide—follower of the seven laws of Noah.

Nudnik (also spelled noodnik)—Yiddish, although it can mean a boring person, it usually refers to someone who is a "pain in the butt."

Orthodox Judaism—the strictest branch of Judaism. Halacha is binding as are the 613 mitzvot.

Parve (also spelled pareve)—neither milk nor meat. Eggs and fish, however, are considered parve as are plant products.

Passover—see Pesach.

Pesach—a seven or eight day (in Diaspora) holiday in Nisan when it is forbidden to eat leavened products. Furthermore, Ashkenazi Jews tend to avoid rice, corn, peanuts, and legumes (beans) and possibly other items.

Prophets—when referring to the Hebrew Bible this includes Joshua, Judges, both books of Samuel, both books of Kings, Isaiah, Heremiah, Ezekiel, the Twelve Prophets which include Hosea, Joel, Amos, Obadiah, Jonah, Micah, Nahum, Habakkuk, Zephaniah, Haggai, Zechariah, and Malachi.

Purim—a celebratory religious festival commemorating the victory of the Jewish people over Haman as told in the book of Esther. Held on Adar 14, or in leap years on the 14th day of Adar II. In cities that were walled during the time of Joshua, Shushan Purim is held on the 15th day of Adar or Adar II (in leap years).

Purim dePrazos—the name given to the day prior Shushan Purim, corresponds to Adar 14, which is the date Purim is celebrated in Diaspora.

Purim Katan—during leap years, this occurs on Adar 14 in the first month of Adar.

Purim Meshulash—a rare occurrence when Shushan Purim falls on Shabbat causing Purim to be three days long. This is the name of the third day of the festival but is also used for the festival as a whole.

Reform Judaism—the largest movement of liberal Judaism. Halacha is considered non-binding and is interpreted more as a set of general guidelines to how to live a Jewish life. As halacha is considered non-binding, it is easily changeable and modernized.

Right of Return—the laws by which individuals can make aliyah. If someone would have been persecuted as a Jew under the Nazi regime, they are qualified to move to Israel provided they do not practice a religion other than Judaism. Individuals who have at least one Jewish parent or grandparent, are married to Jews, or are converts to Judaism may apply to make aliyah to Israel. Even liberal Jewish converts may make aliyah thanks to the Miller Precedent.

Rosh—"Head." As in the Rosh Beit Din is the head of the Beit Din, the sponsoring rabbi in a conversion. Also in Rosh Hashanah, "head of the year." The first of every month is also called "Rosh."

Rosh Hashanah—"head of the year." Also the Day of Judgment.

Seder—means "order" and usually made in reference to a ritual meal.

Sephardic Jews—"Spanish Jews." Generally considered to be most of the Jewish community around the Mediterranean. This is the second-largest Jewish ethnicity.

Sevivon—Hebrew word referring to what is commonly more known by its Yiddish name, dreidel.

Seven Species—the seven species are wheat, barley, grape, fig, pomegranates, olive, and dates.

Shabbat—Jewish Sabbath, occurs starting Friday night eighteen minutes before sunset and continues for twenty-five hours until Havdalah. There are thirty-nine categories of work prohibited on Shabbat.

Shamash—helper candle used to light the other candles during Hanukkah.

Shalom bayit—literally Peace [at] Home.

Shavuot—a holiday celebrating the giving of the Torah at Mount Sinai. It is also one of three harvest festivals.

Shehecheyanu—a blessing said for new and rare occasions. In transliterated Hebrew, it is written Baruch atah Adonai Eloheinu Melech ha'olam shehecheyanu, vekiymanu, vehigiyanu lazman hazeh.

Shema (also spelled Shma)—The Jewish declaration of faith. In transliterated Hebrew, it is written: Shema Yisrael, Adonai Eloheinu, Adonai Echad.

Shiur (plural shiurim)—a Talmudic study session.

Shomer Shabbat—strictly observant of Shabbat. There are thirty-nine categories of activities forbidden on Shabbat and people who are Shomer Shabbat will do their best to avoid all of them.

Shtar Giur—certificate of conversion.

Shul—Yiddish for synagogue/school. One of many words used to describe a Jewish house of worship. This is more likely to be used by Jews of Ashkenazi descent.

Shushan Purim—Purim in cities which were walled during the time of Joshua. It is held on the 15th day of Adar or Adar II (in leap years).

Shushan Purim Katan—during leap years, this occurs on Adar 15 in the first month of Adar.

Siddur—prayer book.

Siman Tov—"Good signs." Also the name of a song very commonly sung at joyful occasions.

Shofar—long hollowed out Ram's horn blown primarily on Rosh Hashanah.

Sukkah (or Succah)—temporary dwelling used during the harvest festival of Sukkot.

Sukkot (or Sukkos in Ashkenazi pronunciation)—Festival of booths that reminds us of the temporary dwellings that the Israelites used during their wandering in the desert. It is also one of three pilgrimage festivals. Sukkot lasts for seven days in Israel and eight days in Diaspora.

Synagogue—from Greek, currently one of many words used to describe a Jewish house of worship.

Ta'anit Bechorot—Fast of the first-born, generally occurs on the Eve of Passover.

Ta'anit Esther—Fast of Esther which generally occurs on Adar 13 except when Adar 13 is Shabbat, then it is on Adar 11. During leap years, this is held during Adar II.

Tallit (or tallis in Ashkenazi pronunciation)—a four fringed prayer shawl worn during morning prayers. It is traditionally made out of wool.

Talmud—the oral Torah, there are two of them: the Jerusalem Talmud and the Babylonian Talmud. The Babylonian Talmud is much larger and was written down during the exile to Babylon.

Tanakh—The Hebrew Bible which includes the Torah, Prophets, and Writings.

Tefillin—a biblically mandated mitzvot that requires two black leather boxes attached to leather straps all made from a kosher animal, both boxes include passages from Exodus and Deuteronomy.

Temple—varies depending on the context. Historically, it could be used to refer to the First Temple or Second Temple in Jerusalem. However, it can also be used to describe a Jewish house of worship, usually a Reform house of worship.

Tisha B'Av—saddest day on Jewish calendar, a fast day commemorating basically every bad thing that has ever happened to the Jewish people.

Three Weeks—a period of ever intensifying mourning that starts with the fast of Tammuz (17th of Tammuz) and ending with Tisha B'Av.

Torah—the first five books of Moses: Genesis, Exodus, Leviticus, Numbers, and Deuteronomy.

Tu B'Shevat—New year for the counting of the trees, it is also considered a kabbalistic holiday. It is held on the 15th day of Shevat.

Tzedakah—roughly considered to be the equivalent of charity in English, but the real meaning goes beyond this and is closer in meaning to justice. Every Jew is ritually obliged to give 10% of their income to tzedakah as well as to perform acts of charity.

Tzitzit—fringes won on clothing with four corners, these fringes representing the 613 mitzvot.

Tzom Gedaliah—minor fast day right after Rosh Hashanah.

Tzom Tammuz—a minor fast day on the 17th of Tammuz.

Writings—in the Hebrew Bible, the Writings include the Psalms, Proverbs, Job, Song of Songs, Ruth, Lamentations, Ecclesiastes, Esther, Daniel, Ezra-Nehemiah, and Chronicles (I & II).

Yamim Noraim—another name for the Days of Awe or Days of Repentance. See Days of Awe.

Yarmulke—head covering generally worn by men, although women may wear one if they wish in liberal circles. It is the same as the word kippah.

Yiddish—language spoken by Ashkenazi Jews, it is a high-German dialect.

Yom HaAtzma'ut—Israeli Independence Day.

Yom HaShoah—Holocaust Remembrance Day.

Yom HaZikaron—Day of Remembrance for Israeli Fallen Soldiers and Victims of Terrorism.

Yom Kippur—Day of Atonement, the last of the Days of Awe. The day is marked by a complete twenty-five-hour fast.

Yom Tov—holiday.

Yom Yerushalayim—Jerusalem Day.

Zeroa—roasted lamb or goat bone on a Seder plate. Some vegetarians replace this with a beet.

Zionist—a supporter of Israel.

Printed in the USA
CPSIA information can be obtained
at www.ICGtesting.com
LVHW092354270224
773016LV00032B/386